Reinvent Your Career

Shweta Bhatia

TESTIMONIALS

I have worked with Shweta and have been a friend for many years. I can honestly say she is a dedicated leader, mother and mentor. Her experiences and career growth really makes her an expert in reinventing her brand. While making career changes during her employment journey, she has developed relationships and built a strong brand that has enabled her to achieve executive leadership roles for a fortune 1 company. I am proud of what she has done and that she is my friend. I am very happy that she is sharing her journey and thoughts for all to grow with.

~ Jeff Gorman - Retail Executive

I have known Shweta for 7 years. We started as colleagues but have evolved to much more than that over the years because of the connection we have and the deep sense of admiration for each other.

I remember when I met Shweta the first time in the lobby of our California office. She was traveling from Wisconsin and very humbly she told me that she had helped launch the pilot for our first omni initiative which I knew had also been scaled to half the fleet of stores. Only later I realized what a ground breaking accomplishment it was for our company as it unleashed an era of transformation as it relates to brick and mortar stores becoming one with our digital channels.

From that point on, she went on push the envelope on several key initiatives for the company. If I were to summarize Shweta's skills in 4 words: She can move mountains .. and make it look effortless. Ok that was more than 4 but you get the idea!

You are probably thinking may be it wasn't so hard. It was HARD. There were challenges at every corner. Typical office politics, ambiguity, risks and unknowns. She led her teams fearlessly, confidently and more importantly .. with honesty and humility. Regardless of what came here way, she made sure that she enjoyed the journey more than chasing the destination.

She is a great leader - one of the very few women leaders that I genuinely admire and look up to.

This is her story and offers a valuable perspective on how to succeed. I would highly recommend this book to anyone who wants to grow as a leader and a person!

~ Garima Agarwal - Technology Executive & Author

Why do I often feel like am hitting against dead wall? Why are my efforts unnoticed and unrecognized by people that matter for my career growth? I shed my blood, sweat, and tears to accomplish a critical project at my work and I still didn't attain the promotion I was looking for.

These are the challenges most of us come across in our rut of corporate careers. The author, Shweta Bhatia brings forth decades of learnings, impactful stories, simple tips that should inspire you, challenge you, encourage you, and correct you towards a much more rewarding career outcome!

~ Hari Kandalam - Technology Executive

In this game changing book Shweta shares some of the processes she has used in her own career and in coaching others. I can personally attest to her amazing character and ability to guide others. She has shown me I am capable of doing more than I ever thought I could. I am a better leader and person because of her. In this book Shweta brilliantly outlines the rainbow process to share many of the key things that can help everyone to live a fulfilling career and life.

~ Melissa Roth - Mentee

As an Executive coach, I have coached hundreds of leaders and Shweta stands out a true top leader. She has a deep care for her work, her people and for the impact she's making in the world. But what takes her to the next level of extraordinary leadership is her wisdom. Every conversation includes numerous pieces of wisdom that I find myself stopping to capture. Because of this natural talent, there's no one better suited to be sharing her knowledge and experience on how to "Reinvent Your Career." I'm thrilled that this book will help so many people create more fulfilling personal and professional lives.

~ Heidi Kraft, Leadership Alchemist - Kraft Your Success

Having worked with Shweta in an executive role, the guidance she shares are also the footsteps she walks. Applying her simple and well developed framework, you'll instantly feel much more confident in pursuing your vision. This book cuts straight to the chase on what you need to do to make the most of the opportunities that come your way and more importantly, to live a fulfilling life.

What a fantastic, straightforward and honest book. I'll be recommending it to everyone who has aspirations, but needs a little help to achieve their goals. Simple, concise and worth reading twice.

~ Brian Dennis - Customer Experience Keynote Speaker and Best Selling Author

I had the good fortune of working with Shweta to learn how to transform personal and professional life. The approach she coached is practical advice. I have already benefited from Brand Management. It plays a significant role in portraying what you do concisely. Shweta also have a gift for discussing interactions in truthful yet amusing ways. It seems I can always identify experiences around me with those you describe. It made me realize that our problems are typical, and we can solve them in constructive ways. You pointed out several things that I will remember and implement for years to come.

~ Sundar - Mentee

Shweta is a passionate learner, curious about the connectivity of all things she touches, directly or indirectly in her work. She has intellectual stamina and discipline to push through ambiguity, lead change and bring teams of people along. Her book unlocks powerful insights for those who find themselves in career transitions, or merely at 'stuck' points in their journey of fulfillment. Shweta's insights are authentic, derived from her experience. A worthy read from a truly remarkable person.

₋₁ **Michael Donohue   Retail Executive**

DEDICATION

To my parents, whom I shall remain indebted for giving me a chance to see the world in my own way and for believing in me.

To my husband, Mayank, who is my biggest supporter and worst critic.

To my daughter, Tanya, to my son, Yuvraj, who have been my coaches throughout my life.

CONTENTS

Chapter 1: Own Your Power   1

Chapter 2: Master Belief in Yourself; Things   9
Will Follow if You Just Believe

Chapter 3: The Beginning of Your   21
Transformation Journey Starts with the
RAINBOW Process

Chapter 4: Personal Brand Management   27

Chapter 5: Storytelling – Offer Your Unique   37
Story

Chapter 6: Authentic Networking And   51
Relationship Building

Chapter 7: Listening to Intuition   63

Chapter 8: Resilience, Adapting to Change,   73
And Perseverance

Chapter 9: EQ Is Far More Important Than IQ   93

Chapter 10: Ways of Living   103

Chapter 11: Crafting The RAINBOW of Life   113

Acknowledgments   121

About the Author   125

CHAPTER ONE: OWN YOUR POWER

Monica came from humble beginnings. She set lofty goals with her untamed soul and burning desire to stand on her own two feet and become an independent working professional. She has had dreams since she was a young child. Her ambition was to create a unique identity and be the best version of herself.

She had a decent start in her life after completing her undergraduate and graduate programs. She was focused and a visionary. She progressed in her career primarily due to her core talent, competence, and immense hard work, but as she moved up the ladder into middle management, she found herself stuck, struggling with career advancements and overall growth. Monica believed she had done everything she could think of, but apparently, what got her this far was not helping her any further. What brought her to this point was primarily her hard work, impeccable work ethic, and prioritizing work over other things in life, which served her well until this point. Clearly, the recipe of early career progression was somehow stale, given that she was in the next stage.

Monica came to the brutal realization that not everything was hunky-dory and as easy as she first thought in her early career days. She found herself in a conundrum. She pondered whether the decisions she was making would fulfill her ambitions. The spark that would light her up and make her wake up every morning, challenging her to seize the world and every opportunity that came her way. Her myths were royally busted as she tried to find the lost part of herself. Her figment of imagination followed, "Just work hard, and rest everything will follow." No doubt, the core philosophy remained true, but a lot more was needed to achieve her goals. She needed to gather clarity, and security, to enable her to live a fulfilled, happy life. She always aspired to rise high in her professional field of play, but this figment of imagination clouded her path. She transitioned into a new phase of life where her career was a dominating factor. She felt trapped and realized that time was slipping out of her hands, that whatever got her so far in her career had been exhausted and that she needed a new toolkit. She desperately needed a new set of values and strategies to give her a push toward her dream. She was unaware of all the parts required in the sausage-making for personal and professional growth. This feeling had taken a significant toll on her life; she was mentally and emotionally exhausted. She'd often imagine herself quitting and questioning: IS IT ALL WORTH IT? It was unbearably painful to see her dreams shattered and live an unfulfilled life.

Monica drifted further away from her life's objective with every passing day. Every day for her seemed like a chore; it was a struggle to wake up when there was so little to look forward to. She grew anxious, which impacted her health and relationship with her spouse, children, and most importantly, herself. The gradual collapse of development in her career was beyond her scope of comprehension and severed her connection with herself. Staying where she was, Monica was not only limiting her career development and progression, but her confidence level was deteriorating by the day.

She felt hurt, confused, mad, sad, glad, depressed, mad again, joyful, panicked, emotional, pitiful, sick, elated, content—if you can name an emotion, she's felt it—more than once. She went through several emotionally overwhelming episodes during which she self-analyzed her capabilities and questioned her self-worth in aspects of her professional being. She had doubts about her skills and abilities, the same skills she once took pride in. She often downplayed her skills and knowledge and over-thought every situation, which led to a distorted self-image. Monica demeaned her work and sought validation from others, as a consequence of which she lost her confidence. She often compared her mortified self to others whose journey seemed glorious, which made her lose her confidence even further.

Monica was at a disadvantage because of a lack of significant engagement and associations within the organization that included mentors, advocates, and sponsors who could have encouraged and facilitated improvements in her career development. She did not have a trusted coach or partners who could help chart her future. She did not have a godfather or a champion in the organization. She did not know who her allies were and lacked a well-defined identity.

All of this led to daily excruciating mental anguish, detrimental to her living state. It seemed like work had taken over her life. All of that led to "burnout."

Clearly, Monica was going through a midlife career crisis and could not see the light at the end of the tunnel.

In this world, everything gets created twice: first in your mind and then in the real world. Often, we live as prisoners of our minds, thereby shying away from exercising judgment in favor of the less-traveled path in life. Your mind can hold you hostage, unknown to you. Your thoughts and beliefs control your entire life. Beliefs are what we ultimately have a choice over. The belief of self-doubt, unworthiness that I am not good enough, the belief of having no options, etc. You hold the keys to your freedom because you have locked yourself up. The first step is acknowledging the truth and then seeking help to free yourself.

There will always be someone who has gone through a similar journey as you have and has already experienced and overcome the hard part. The goal is to explore more, encounter individuals who have fought similar battles through their careers, or learn about similar events, whichever would lead you to your ultimate goal. It is easier said than done, but taking a step forward today is the key.

The absence of self-assurance and faith in your potential happens ordinarily due to the lack of a good enough toolkit that helps people face challenges head-on. It is neither taught in any institution nor defined in any current framework. I have acquired some of these career survival skills through my experiences, and this is a heartfelt attempt to help people with aspirations who are facing this challenge day in and day out.

When I started my journey, I faced numerous challenges of varying degrees. When dealing with success, one should not forget the battle necessary for triumph and the emotional turmoil that comes along with it. I was not sufficiently loaded with opportunities as I was not born with a silver spoon. Hence, whatever knowledge I absorbed and the fundamental values

4

I learned that shaped my character came from excruciating processes and demanding tasks. Therefore, it can be safely deduced that I have been in similar situations as you, and I see parts of myself in you every day. This epiphany inspired me to provide you with a toolkit and articulate methods to assist you on your journey to living an enriched and fulfilled life.

Thank God for the path clearers and creators. I have been grateful to these angels in my life, and nothing beats human inspiration when your ultra lazy and risk-averse brain is trying to find reasons for "WHY DO IT?" Such examples define models of success and command the "indolent and addicted to the comforts of life" mind that "It is possible to take risks, pursue goals, and that there is substantial proof of success." When you are firmly convinced that certain things are impractical and impossible, you may rarely have met someone audacious who has already accomplished these things magnificently. It is entirely normal to be baffled, perplexed, and mystified. It's OK to ask. It's OK to say, "I don't know." It's OK to seek help from the path's creators.

In this business world where every individual wants a taste of success at any cost, it is often effective and enriching to learn from others' wisdom and experiences rather than go through the vicious cycle all by yourself. It is painful and expensive in every aspect—emotional, mental, social, psychological, physical, etcetera. It is generally a strenuous process that one must avoid. When we tag people as geniuses, we often forget that the greatest in the world follow a set of routines that allow them to deliver at peak performance every time. It is the little, simple things done with utmost discipline that one must perfect and continue to do even when no one is looking.

Writer Annie Dillard famously said, "How we spend our days is, of course, how we spend our lives." The majority of us spend a significant portion of our days at work; in fact, the average person works 90,000 hours in their lifetime.

It is safe to say that your job and work environment can considerably impact the quality of your life, empowering you to live a life full of joy, happiness, and contentment.

Several studies suggest a strong interdependency between personal and work life. Monica's professional life seriously impacted her personal life, and resolving her career crisis would likely cure what ails her.

When Monica saw the light at the end of the tunnel and came out of her midlife career catastrophe, she felt liberated. She not only had a path to achieve her professional goals, but she started living a fulfilling life on all fronts—emotional, mental, psychological, physical, spiritual, social, and financial. She attained clarity, regained her confidence, and developed a stronger belief in herself. Monica was engaged and happy and had overcome her fears to achieve success in her professional life. She felt valued and didn't stop there; she continued stronger than ever before. She now shows up to every conversation with gravitas, confidence, and a great presence.

She owns her power. I know this about her because I, too, have been there.

CHAPTER TWO: MASTER BELIEF IN YOURSELF; THINGS WILL FOLLOW IF YOU JUST BELIEVE

"Nothing is more powerful than a made up mind – nothing. Period."
~ Shweta Bhatia

Growing up in a middle-class family in India and coming from humble origins, I realized early on in my life that I needed to lean in and envision the future I wanted for myself. I grew up in a developing country where boys were typically given preference over girls in almost every aspect of life, particularly in careers and workplaces. Fortunately, I was born into a family not stuck in traditional taboos and societal stereotypes. However, seeing the inequality between men and women around me and the lack of cerebral opportunities for women fueled a deep sense of anguish. That morphed into a fierce desire and propensity for hard work to accomplish something in life, not only for myself but also for the women deprived of a successful and independent life.

Gender disparity in our society was excruciatingly painful. Mostly, I encountered men in positions of power and influence, which fueled my desire more. I always wondered, about the fact that highly influential and dignified jobs, "WHY CAN'T I?" What is making me and other females incompetent for the same positions in the hierarchy? The complexity and understanding of this thought were beyond my scope of comprehension. All that raw energy channeled itself and made me envision a great future for myself. I knew what I did not want my future to be from the initial stage, which helped me visualize my next step better. I had big dreams, wanted to go places, and did not want to receive "no" as an answer at any point in time.

There were 5.3 billion people on the planet back then, but only one me. I wanted to create the most unique and fantastic version of myself based on my values, beliefs, vision, dreams, and passions, making my unique path and road map. I did not care what other people thought of me, and I surely did not hesitate to take risks. Despite all the social pressure to take on the medical profession or pursue administrative services, I pinned my mind on doing a master's in business administration. When most of my classmates opted for the stereotypical choices, I trusted my intuition.

Though I did not have much guidance on planning and executing my career path, I had unconditional support from my parents to pursue my dreams of becoming the best version of myself. I was fortunate to have parents who treated me as a thoughtful person from a young age. I was a determined, gregarious young soul who wanted to change the stereotypes and challenge the former arbitrary and discriminatory system. I am appreciative and indebted to my parents for having played a crucial role in shaping the person I am today. They believed in me, trusted my choices, and supported me regardless of the repercussions of my decisions. They were my confidantes and pillars of strength. My parents gave me the freedom to express my opinions and views on critical decisions and essential matters, which helped me build high self-esteem.

The excerpt includes a description of the time during a summer break when I was in seventh grade. I wanted to visit my grandparents, who lived five states and 300 miles away. I insisted that I travel by myself via train to cover a twelve-hour journey where I had to switch trains in between. There were no mobile phones at that time; the only way to communicate with my parents about my well-being was when I arrived at my grandparents' house. I somehow persuaded my parents that I would be safe, but only I knew how terrified I was. I was petrified from within but eagerly wanted to experience the adventures of traveling alone. I saw myself curled up in the train cabin with a lot of fear and belief combined. I was the only thirteen-year-old by myself in the train compartment and naturally stood out. I had to portray myself in a certain way to make it not look obvious that I was internally gutted and scared. Anyhow, I made it through. The whole experience felt like climbing Mount Everest.

A couple of months later, during a conversation with my mother, she asked, "How did the train ride feel?"

I answered, "It was terrifying yet amazing." I thoroughly enjoyed the experience and became stronger within.

And then she asked, "How many children were like you on the train?"

"None," I replied. Everyone had an adult accompanying them.

She said, "How many children are getting this kind of

opportunity like you?"

I said, "I don't think there are many."

She said, "You know how much I love you, and it took a lot of courage for me to allow this. But I did not send you to have an independent train ride. I sent you there to see what the world was like and be ready for it, and I am so proud. The world will not necessarily be fair, and the world may not necessarily like you, but you need to gather the courage and get out there, live it for yourself, know how to stand up for yourself, and be okay." It was a tough lesson to learn, but it was necessary.

The train ride taught me invaluable and crucial life skills that have been a catalyst in my professional journey. I gained a sense of independence and an "I can do anything" mindset; it taught me to be comfortable with taking risks, helped build the unquenchable curiosity muscle, and developed the courage to navigate on my own, to be comfortable in unknown territory. I learned that it is okay not to know everything and embrace ambiguity and vulnerability, which equates to more confidence. It was not easy, but it was the smartest thing to learn. It gave me the confidence that I could achieve anything if I put my mind to it. This lesson has served me tremendously to date, and I hope it always will. I completed my MBA from a good school, and I went to start living my dreams. All these years, I have faced several challenges. The only thing that kept me going was a laser focus on the life I had envisioned for myself—nothing else.

Mind Over Everything

"Envision your future. Draw it out and think it out loud. It will eventually become a part of your DNA. Listen to your heart and do what feels right. "
~ Shweta Bhatia

Life is messy a lot of the time. Success is even more chaotic. My first job as an intern was to build web content for an online start-up to sell liquor online. I knew absolutely nothing about the business, nor did I understand any basics about the product line. I came from a family where alcohol was considered taboo. To do the job I was hired for, I had to visit multiple bars to interview the owners, bartenders, and customers; it was a different experience. I, yet again, brutally noticed the lack of social equity between men and women. To prove myself, I had to put in more effort and work much harder than my male colleagues – volunteered or not. Although I did not cherish or appreciate my first working experience, since I had no other option, I had to reap whatever little benefits of the job.

In this three-month gig, I felt cringed up, embarrassed, and ashamed. India is known to have a deep sense of culture intertwined with social taboos. I was wrapped within the misogynistic undertones, and through this experience, I realized there would be moments in life where I would waste my time on ideas that looked dumb at the time, moments where I would get distracted and waste more time. Still, it was all a part of the journey. The key question was: how long do I stick with something that will not align with my core values and purpose? It did not connect with my purpose, and only lasted three months. I listened to my heart and left a well-paying job.

Magic happens when you listen to your heart, and your piles of mistakes transform into massive successes. Acknowledge and learn from these experiences and relish the journey.

When in doubt during uncertain situations—ask yourself—"What's the worst possible outcome?"

I then moved to the United States, my heart filled with dreams and aspirations. I was nervous and exhilarated. I had read that it was a land of opportunities. I truly believed that. I still do. But what I did within the "land of opportunities" was up to me – no one else.

I became an entrepreneur at a young age when I first arrived in the United States after struggling to find work due to the lack of a work permit. I tried for a long time to get into the workforce before someone saw the spark in me and offered me a job, only to make me their partner in a short time. I wasn't sure if I had the capability to take on this role. There were numerous times when I was overwhelmed, had self-doubt, and did not think I could survive. Taking each day as it came, second-guessing on-the-fly decisions, and not knowing what I was doing most of the time. It wasn't that we were doing a lousy job; it was crucial because many people's lives depended on us. Being an entrepreneur involves substantial responsibility and accountability.

There were days I could barely breathe, but I just kept swimming every time I felt trapped and suffocated. I thought I could not hold the burden anymore and would collapse at any time. I was eagerly waiting to leave the room and catch a breath. It was then that I remembered the most practical advice my father had given me: "Keep moving forward." When patience is wearing thin, taking minuscule, tiny steps one at a time helps.

It became my guidepost when I desperately wanted to give up. Just one more step was my mantra. The only way to get through challenging times was to show up regardless of the noise. I had to instill a little more faith each day. I had a fantastic time riding the crazy wave, knocking me down so often and leaving me breathless. At the same time, I learned and overcame several barriers, such as cultural, language, social, and economic, to name a few. Being thousands of miles away from my family was hard at times, but the spark within me kept me going.

The vision of going after what I wanted, to be the best version of myself, to combat the fears that I had set for myself early on in my life, was my light and guidepost.

"I realized the risk wasn't that bad, and I had nothing to lose when I started." Say yes to opportunities and then figure it out; you will. "Leave your comfort zone, no matter how uncomfortable it might feel."
~Shweta Bhatia

There are some moments in life that give you cues to pivot. Something similar once happened to me; my daughter, who was a toddler back then, clung to me and cried for thirty whole minutes after I returned from a work trip. That was a pivotal moment for me. It made me reflect and internalize the purpose of my life. I took a moment to step back and reflect on what had just happened. It helped me gain perspective and a deeper understanding of what truly mattered and was important in life. After deep reflection, it became clear to me. Traveling three to four days per week was exhausting for her and I. She could not say it that well, but she figured out her way of expressing it, which worked miraculously. I could deeply feel and sense what my child was going through internally without her saying a word. I am so grateful for that moment. It was one of the best moments because I decided to prioritize my personal life over my professional life, and my teenage daughter is now my best friend. I would have missed a lot in life had I not made that pivot. When we fail to pause and reflect on our lives, we lose perspective and often lose sight of the most important things. It was then that I decided to make a pivot in my professional life.

It was a life-changing event to go from being an entrepreneur to entering the corporate world. It felt like moving a fish from a lake to a pond. You call the shots when you are an entrepreneur, so the shift was quite dramatic. Despite all the anticipated challenges and cons associated with the change, I could only profoundly feel my daughter's unexpressed pain, which was the only thing that mattered. My husband and I debated this for several weeks—the pros, cons, and everything. He held his ground that the transition would be overwhelming with unexpected twists and turns that might consume all my grit. He supported my decision wholeheartedly but with some genuine skepticism. It was not only my husband; others had the same concerns. As I went through the interview process, the last round of interviews was with the head of the department. He was supposed to interview me for forty-five minutes, but it lasted for ninety, as he wasn't wholly convinced that I would stick to the job. He tried hard to talk me out of taking the job. He said, "This is the time to ask for more stake in the company; why are you even thinking of this job?" You will get bored. Well, I had prioritized my personal life over my professional life. I wanted to spend a considerable amount of time raising my daughter, which was non-negotiable. Everything else had to work around that premise.

Starting my corporate world journey seemed unusual and slightly different from being a small company entrepreneur. At first glance, I did not fit in; the new and much larger environment, new groups and people, new community, social environment, and just a lot of unknowns and newness seemed overwhelming. As it's probably true for any large organization, my eyes were opened to the lengthy processes, gyrations of approvals for most things, political nuances, long-standing cohorts that were tough to become a part of, favoritism, biases—a lot was different from a start-up. But hey, that was my decision, and I wanted to give it a serious attempt and went all in without over-analyzing and introspecting. Through this process, I also uncovered my philosophy of "no regrets."

Through my entrepreneurial and corporate journey of twenty years, working for and closely with many Fortune 500 companies, I have had the privilege to learn some fantastic, uncomplicated yet powerful life lessons that go in what I call my RAINBOW BOX. This is my go-to place when I seek inspiration. This is a box where I place my life lessons and learnings to draw from in the future. It provides excellent reflection, and I am grateful for the breadcrumbs I laid out for myself through this rainbow box.

Much like you, I had my share of fears and trepidations. I did not have someone who would be my sponsor, aka godfather. I did not have the conventional pedigree of a start-up founder. I honestly and utterly relied on my gut and did not let my doubts or the doubters hold me back. Often, even the most straightforward and basic tasks felt abnormally exhausting and resulted in an unusually sizable cognitive effort, which resulted in my burnout countless times. As they say, necessity is the mother of invention; this repetitive burnout was the door that led me on my spiritual journey. My heartfelt desire is that I will be able to share the key lessons and a process that may help you in your future endeavors.

"Remember, if you are not uncomfortable, you are not growing."
~Shweta Bhatia

Reinvent Your Career

CHAPTER THREE: THE BEGINNING OF YOUR TRANSFORMATION JOURNEY STARTS WITH THE RAINBOW PROCESS

You feel stuck and are miserable, disappointed with yourself, and unable to progress in your professional life. You have come to the realization that not everything is hunky-dory as you thought early on in your career. Your myths around development, learning, and growth are busted. You are leading a disenchanted and frustrating life because a good part of your life revolves around your profession.

If all of this sounds familiar and resonates with you and your life, there is a high probability that you are going through a midlife career crisis.

We are living in ever-changing and disruptive times. Winston Churchill famously said, "If you are going through hell, keep going."

But the real question is, how does one prepare?

Life happens, continuing to amaze and astound us with its colors, some good and some not so good. There will be highs and lows. How do you prepare to catch the curveballs? The best way to prepare is to proactively and intentionally disrupt yourself every day, even just a little. My intent is to help you create your RAINBOW. Remember, life is not just about reaching your goal; it is the journey you embark upon and how you grow as you move towards it.

I have gone through the same excruciating struggles in my more than twenty years of professional life, and my dream is for you to have a significant mindset change by going through this process. You will feel energized, motivated, and confident, and you will attain clarity to build a plan to achieve your professional goals and live a fulfilled life. You will overcome your inhibitions through this journey.

I have crafted a seven-step framework to help you unleash your true potential through defined micro-steps.

The Seven-Step RAINBOW Process

R: Resilience and adaptability
A: Adapting EQ
I: Intuition
N: Networking
B: Brand management
O: Offer your unique story
W: Ways of living

Resilience, Adapting to Change, and Perseverance

By learning to be adaptable, resilient, and perseverant in life, you will envisage that these three are the key competencies you must continuously develop to succeed in your personal and professional life. Your ability to pivot in a dynamic environment quickly is critical to achieving your career goals and living a fulfilled life. If you don't change, you will lose the long-term game.

EQ is Far More Important Than IQ

Embrace and adapt to EQ. Through real-life stories and examining the significance and desideratum of EQ, you will recognize the crucial role EQ plays in your life. You will be able to understand the difference between "What's right" versus "What's right, right now." There are low days in life, but how do you equip yourself to handle them differently? EQ is the muscle you need to build to respond rather than react in situations and make the most out of every situation without feeling aggrieved.

Listening to Intuition

Through my personal experiences in this book, I hope you will gain the courage to listen to your intuition when you find yourself torn between taking chances. When you are in doubt, you will listen to yourself, be able to weigh in on the pros and cons, and be comfortable taking risks while thinking of the long-term game. You will also understand the role intuition plays in hearing what isn't said.

Authentic Networking and Relationship Building

Having the right people around you at the right time works wonders. There is a greater chance that there will always be someone who did the hard part. The key is to explore around you to find them and build life-long, authentic relationships. At the end of this chapter, you will understand the role trusted relationships and networking play in your personal and professional life. Nothing beats human inspiration. You will also get a framework to help with this.

Personal Brand Management

A personal brand is your personal visiting card that never gets printed but is imprinted on you. You carry it with you twenty-four hours a day, seven days a week. In the following chapter, you will understand what a personal brand is, its need, and its significance in your life. You will also get a greater understanding of your current brand and how you can evolve it. Simply put, how would people describe you in less than ten words?

Storytelling: Offer Your Unique Story

We communicate most effectively through sharing stories. Communication through storytelling will teach you how you can leverage storytelling to effortlessly and smoothly communicate in your life, both personally and professionally. Through this step, you will understand the importance of storytelling and will have tips to construct your own story.

Ways of Living

Through my life story, you will be able to see how your head, heart, and hands synchronize, making the journey fulfilling and enjoyable. Your transformation in this digital era requires a holistic, human-centric approach, one I call the "Head, Heart, and Hands" of transformation. Attending to all three elements will enable you to succeed today and thrive tomorrow. Being free and happy comes from a place of peace and being in sync with yourself.

Through this seven-step RAINBOW process, my holy grail for you is to achieve a significant mindset change that thrives on challenges and sees failure as a heartening springboard for growth, sincerely enabling you to be the most authentic version of yourself. You feel energized, motivated, and confident, and gain clarity to become conscientious about creating a plan and achieving your goals. You can overcome your inhibitions through this journey and become unstoppable in anything you set your mind to achieve. You learn how to respond to crucial conversations, handle tough and delicate situations, persist in the face of setbacks, and embrace challenges. You become enriched not only when you reach the end of the RAINBOW, but also throughout your journey, with fulfillment, ultimate success, and by being the courageous and fierce you. Ultimately, you discover your pot of gold throughout this journey.

"It does not matter where you come from, but where you're going."
~Brian Tracy

Reinvent Your Career

26

CHAPTER FOUR: PERSONAL BRAND MANAGEMENT

You might conjecture what personal brand management is and encounter questions: "Do you have a personal brand? How do you know what brand you currently have? Are there steps to reconcile the gaps? How do you build a plan for the brand you want to have for yourself?" I often get asked these questions by the folks I coach.

Your personal brand is your reputation. It is like a visiting card that never gets printed but is imprinted on you. It is how you authentically portray yourself in every setting over a period of time. It is how you show up without concealment and demonstrate your appearance, your fine introduction, your body language and mannerism, and how well prepared you are. Do you radiate a positive aura? Are you inclined to listen to different ideas and perspectives? It's about how you deal with precarious situations and show off your wits and personality.

This chapter contains cognizance about personal branding and the difference between your perception of yourself and how others perceive you. You will be able to identify the critical gaps between internal and external images. You will learn and unlearn various fundamental facts to build your brand. It will help you provide building blocks and a practical framework to unlock a window, a door, or a gate preventing you from building a strong brand for yourself. I want you to picture the person you want to emulate and gain the confidence to excel in building your brand. I will encapsulate the struggles I dealt with early on in my career due to my lack of understanding and how my personal brand played a crucial role in my life.

If someone asks you, "What is your personal brand?" more often than not you will find it tremendously challenging to counter and contemplate. What does "personal brand" signify? This is precisely how I felt when my boss asked me the aforementioned during a developmental conversation. I thought I was doing great and walked on water, ready for the next step in my career, but this caught me off-guard. I was perceived as incapable of doing the job. Mind you, this was not even a promotion or compensation change, it was a scope change. Even then, my perception played a critical role. To my surprise, I was confused and did not know the difference between self-image and personal brand. I thought how I saw myself was exactly how others saw me too. I was naive and highly disappointed in myself. I was disgruntled and disengaged for a long time. This led to self-doubt and low confidence. I had to go through the trenches of self-reflection and pull myself back up to accept the reality that there is a remarkable difference between self-image and your personal brand. Self-image is how you see yourself; your personal brand is how others see you.

Building your brand does not magically happen overnight. It requires you to identify your non-negotiable core values. It then takes intentionality:

- You are soliciting feedback about yourself from others around you (both personal and professional people).
- You are open to feedback.
- You are reflecting upon that feedback.
- You are intentionally acting on it.
- Soliciting feedback again
- Repeating the process.

Much like yourself, your personal brand is a work in progress—it needs work.

At the end of the day, how would people describe you in less than ten words? What are the key adjectives others will use when they think of you?

If you don't define your personal brand, it will be defined for you—the choice is yours.

Think of both a person and a company you would consider to have a strong brand, and why you picked them? Please take out your journal and write down:

Person:

Company:

There must be some core values as to why you picked the names. Perhaps trust, innovation, power, commitment, or honesty, to name a few. However, the consistency in their behavior when the core values were repeated time and time again and the persistence in their character resonated and stuck with you. Consistently living the core values every day plays a crucial role in building a strong personal brand; that's precisely why you picked the person and the company you did. It is due to the consistency they demonstrate.

How to Start This Process

Here are a few key elements that are essential to building your brand:

1. Identify your non-negotiable core values fundamental to your existence and purpose.

2. Assessment –

    A. Conduct an internal review with yourself—what are the key attributes you exhibit?

    B. Conduct an external review with your family and immediate companions—what strengths do they recognize in you?

    C. Conduct an external review with your colleagues—what strengths do they identify in you?

    D. How do online researchers define your character?

Your current brand image summarizes what you learned from the above exercise (A-D).

    E. You can identify the gaps by subtracting how you see yourself from others.

3. Think about your core values and what you need to do to fill in the gaps and learn the skills you don't already have.

    A. Your career plan needs to be in alignment with your core values. Integrating your actions with your core values will enhance and continue to build your brand.

4. Outline a plan to build those skills.

5. Your future brand evolution starts here.

As you are working on this five-step process, remember to have a "purpose filter" – ask yourself a set of probing questions (such as: is this who I am from the core, will I be true to my authentic self, etcetera) to stay true to your purpose. Be great at saying "no" if something doesn't align with your brand and purpose.

Critical Elements to a Personal Brand

1. Professional Appearance

First impressions last for a long time, if not forever. A dear mentor turned friend told me that when you are in leadership roles, you are on display at all times. Everything you do is observed and noted by leaders and teams who look at you. Please don't underestimate the importance of how this can be instrumental in building your brand without you realizing it. Don't dress for your job; dress for the job you want. The "dressing" is just a metaphor for demeanor: how you communicate, exhibit professionalism while eating, following dining etiquette, etc. Simply put, developing your personal image is important so that people you meet and interact with will get positive perceptions of you.

2. Do you appear confident in yourself?

Confidence is a fickle little thing. It's so easy to put your self-esteem in the hands of others when it should only be up to you. The good news is that you're in charge of this self-assurance train, and it's about to leave the station. If you know you look like a confident, capable person, you'll eventually start to feel like one too.

3. How do you Interact in Meetings - do you Respond to Situations Versus React?

While reactions can be instinctive, powerful, and quick, it is always important to read the situation, think about what could happen, weigh the pros and cons, and develop the best argument and solution for the predicament.

4. Do you Listen to Understand or Listen Only to Respond?

Being mindfully present, observing the space, and comprehending the context, rather than listening only to prepare a quick response and blurt out the first thoughts, demonstrates that you are unskillful and emotionally triggered.

5. Are you Followed and Understood - do you Speak at a Reasonable Pace?

Taking a couple of seconds for yourself, aligning your thoughts, pausing to take a quick breather, labeling your reactions mindfully, and responding thoughtfully step by step, while keeping yourself collected throughout the conversation, will better impact others.

These fundamental elements will help you construct a personal brand for yourself. Developing your personal image will build your reputation, creating your mark for the outside world and marketing yourself as an individual. Personal brand management is not about carving a new personality but rather focusing on your authentic self. The aforementioned steps will help you highlight your true strengths.

Finally, begin writing your professional introduction using the guidelines and framework outlined above.

On a sheet of paper or in your journal, finish the following sentences:

- I am a…
- I am known for…
- What this means to me is…
- I have done this for…

It won't be faultless the first time. Let's be honest — it will be a shabby first draft. However, it will evolve to be a great and prominent introduction as you work through this process.

My brand's evolution: As I went through this facade, I saw my brand gradually improving. As it evolved, I went from being result-driven to a thoughtful, strategic leader who deeply cared about people while driving business results. It took a long time and a lot of hard work, but it was worth it in the long run.

You now have an insight into what a personal brand is, its

principles, and strategies for building your own. Making a commitment to your evolution and embodying faith will create many extraordinary changes in your life. My desire is for you to build a prominent and successful brand for yourself through this process. Although it may appear extremely difficult at times, I am grateful that you are on this journey. While it's important to do the work, sharing your work is just as important. The next step in the RAINBOW process is an excellent lead-in to that. Storytelling is one of the most powerful ways to breathe life into your brand. How do you build your brand using storytelling?

CHAPTER FIVE: STORYTELLING – OFFER YOUR UNIQUE STORY

During an interview of mine almost a decade ago, one of the best questions asked was, "What's your life story?" versus the generic question of "Tell me something about yourself." The addition of the phrase "life story" changed my narration and response to the question. Life moments become stories, and stories stick. We are all a summation of the micro-stories of our lives. In this chapter, I will show you why stories matter. With that expanded lens, you will be able to put together your life story on a piece of paper. The stories that have defined you so far are the stories you want to write for your future self. You will gain access to a simple framework that will influence your thoughts. You are deeply conditioned to your thinking, and one of the most difficult things you will ever need to change is your mind by changing the pre-existing conditioning of it. How do you tell your mind the stories that have defined you? How do you take inventory of those stories? How do you change the conditioning to build your future life story? What are the stories embedded deep within you that helped you become the person you are today?

We often forget that we constantly attempt to share stories in our life's journeys. Be it to a child, your partner, a colleague, a business partner, a customer, or a friend - just about everyone with whom you interact. I am drawn to people's stories - stories that bring obstacles, accomplishments, and resilience to life. Stories are the best teachers. As the old saying goes, "You don't get a second chance to make a good first impression." It takes seven seconds for people to form a perception about us, and it takes nine interactions to undo it. How are you crafting your story when creating that first impression?

Why are Stories Important?

Let's start by asking ourselves a provocative question. Is there something you cannot use storytelling for?

We all love a good story. We love to read and binge-watch stories. We enjoy the stories that get us to the edge of our seats - those are the movies we remember.

Stories entertain us. Stories move us to tears, change our attitudes, opinions, and behaviors, and inspire us. Stories have a unique ability to build connections. We don't associate feelings with facts, but we will remember the facts if told a story that we can relate and feel connected to. As it turns out, stories also influence the value we put on things. Stories add a lift for no additional investment.

Storytelling has the broadest application in life, personally and professionally. I want to provide you with a story because my leadership style and professional self are compiled from my stories, chapters, and anecdotes. My stories make me who I am today. They made me the leader I am today. Your stories make you who you are, and you should be incredibly proud of those personal narratives, whatever they may be. They have created the person and professional that you are.

(Image A) Your story begins with you. Let's craft your life story on a page, starting from the beginning. In your journal, draw a simple X and Y axis graph. The X-axis is the timeline from the beginning. The Y-axis is where you note the significant positive and negative moments in your life. This view should be a snapshot of the highs and lows in your life journey.

Image A:
(Illustrative)

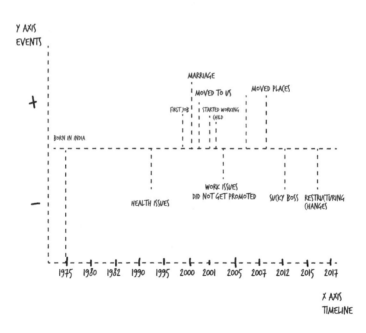

Image B:
(Illustrative)

LEADERSHIP STORY	LIFE STORY (WHAT I LEARNT ABOUT MYSELF)
KEY CAREER MOVES WERE THROUGH MY NETWORK	RISK-TAKER AND MADE GOOD CHOICES IN LIFE
I LOST HOPE WHEN I DIDNT HAVE SUPPORT SYSTEM AT WORK	BOUNCE BACK FROM SETBACKS
NOT AFRAID TO WORK WITH CHALLENGING INDIVIDUALS	FAST LEARNER
	SPIRITUALLY INCLINED

When you go through the exercise of putting your life's highs and lows on a page through retrospection, self-reflection, and soul-searching, you learn quite a bit about yourself; it's a process to discover your own self. When I completed this exercise for myself, I could clearly jot down my leadership story and life story (Image B). I realized my key strengths and the attributes that make me me. Prior to completing this exercise, I'd an idea in my mind, but much needed clarity was provided by writing it down. This was the baseline that helped me craft my future story.

While putting together my story, I forgot several pivotal moments that came to me later. It's astonishing how quickly I moved on with what was going on in the present moment. Putting this together made me take a step back, pause, and reflect on life. It was my life on a single page.

This one-page view of my life helped me learn about myself.

I realized I was a risk-taker; I thrived on challenges and ambiguous situations. I also realized that I needed to get on a spiritual journey to live a truly fulfilling life. As Sir Winston Churchill said, "We make a living by what we get; we make a life by what we give." It gave me a jolt hinting at the missing part of the puzzle.

More importantly, it helped me write a script for my future self.

"It does not matter where you come from, but where you're going."
– Brian Tracy

What is the Future Story You Want to Write?

When I was a child, my father told me a story about his childhood in which he worked the evenings in the theaters to make ends meet for his family. He was only eleven. I can't imagine my eleven-year-old son in the same shoes - my heart clamps even thinking about it. It was a bit after India got its independence, and for my ancestors, it was a survival game. My dad worked evenings and nights and went to school during the day to have a better future. At that time, he wrote his script for his future. The struggles he went through were heartbreaking. However, he broke away from the past, crossed the river, became a civil engineer, supported his extended family, raised three kids, and moved onward. It took a lot of courage to do this. It looks glamorous on paper, but thinking of his story still gives me goosebumps. The only regret he has is that despite receiving admission to a university in California with a hundred percent tuition waiver, he couldn't attend because he couldn't afford the one-way airfare needed to pursue his dream. But hey, perhaps I couldn't have gone as far or accomplished as much as he did and despite facing hardships that could have been roadblocks to pursuing his dreams, my father took charge of writing his own story through perseverance and grit.

What is Your Story?

Action/to-do exercise: Take out your journal and start drawing your life story, comprised of events of the past, scenarios in the present, and goals of the future.

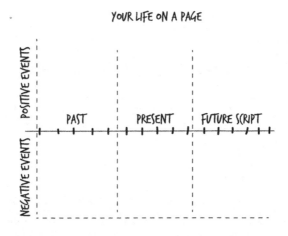

In business, storytelling is as important as having a business plan. Consider every conversation through a storytelling lens as you share a story in every conversation. The most productive and fulfilling discussions you've had were based on sharing stories: stories about your life, children, pet, partner, colleagues, travels, customers, etc. A phone call is a story, putting your toddler to bed is a fairytale, dinner with friends is a story - stories are omnipresent. The same principles apply to your professional life.

The larger the organization, the more critical it becomes to have everyone on the same page through stories.

Well-crafted stories are inspiring, bring people together for a shared vision, help gain cross functional alignment, enable connection with the customer, and help build cross-functional partnerships. Stories provide an alternate way of appealing to emotions when people drown in data and information in today's world. Data-crunching numbers are easy today, extracting and conveying meaning is the difficult part. You extract and share meaningful insight through telling stories.

Storytelling is a relationship strategy—it helps you build trust, everlasting friendships, and connect with people.

Common Mistakes People Make While Telling Stories:

1. Having lack of clarity on why you are telling a story. You need to have clarity on the idea you are trying to sell. Messages become "stickier" when they are wrapped in a story. What impact do you want to create on people? Intentionality is everything.

2. It's all about you. You and your offering are the protagonists in the story.

3. Lack of understanding of who the audience is—what they know, where they are in their journey, and what they are interested in hearing.

4. Avoid sharing the failures and obstacles.

5. Multiple ideas/messages - no one clear message.

6. Size of the prize - "It's not big enough to grab your audience's attention."

7. Lack of relatability - your story is devoid of emotion.

8. It is complicated and hard to follow. Your audience must put in the extra effort to understand.

9. Often, we numb people with numbers—too much data, yet there is no clear insight.

10. Low energy or passion in your story.

Framework and Principles of Storytelling:

1. Know the "why" behind your story.

2. It's not about you, it's about the person you are talking to. The only "superhero" is your customer or your audience. Don't try to be the hero of the stories you tell.

> A. Start with the pattern in the head of the listener and leverage that point to carry the conversation. Do the homework to understand the groove your listener is in.

> B. The basis of every story: how is your listener conceptualizing, and how do you want them to perceive the ambiance through your narrative by the end? What is the listeners' current stance, and where do you want to take them?

3. Stick to one big, bold idea.

4. Outline (upfront) one primary goal you are trying to achieve—is it to inspire, approve, inform, change, or educate?

5. Be human and be vulnerable talk about the failures, the obstacles, the conflicts. It will make your story more credible and engaging.

6. Voice and pitch are powerful instruments of storytelling.

7. Give your audience time to digest and pause. Pace yourself.

8. Keep it simple—don't let your audience do the work. Simple stories are more successful than complicated ones.

9. Close the loop with where you stated. The human mind likes to tie back the end of a story from where it began. Closure will enable your story to stick.

10. Be present in your presentations. No one else will be if you, yourself, are missing.

How to Tell a Good Story

1. Know your purpose, theme, and punchline.

2. Have a top-down approach. Start from a 50,000-foot level and keep making your way down. In the top-down approach, you focus on the macro-level—your story's general feel, shape, and layout. You might start with a map, an economic overview, or the overarching campaign plot, whatever the highest level of your story block is, and work your way down.

3. Have a clear structure.

      A. Beginning, middle, and an end.

      B. Have a simple yet compelling tagline for each transition.

4. Use what you know, and draw from it.

5. Involve your audience in the storytelling—purposefully ask a question. Make it interactive.

6. Be passionate.

7. Be authentic and genuine—show that you care.

Building Your Story Box

You now have your life on a page, your leadership story. The next step is to build your story box with your own inventory of stories. As you leverage storytelling as a critical communication and relationship tool, your story box will be an excellent place to go and draw your stories from. You write stories every day with your family, friends, and colleagues. Keep your story box current with the most vital stories.

Take out your journal and start jotting down your stories to build your story box. Consider the people who have impacted your life: those who have paved the way for you, supported you when you were struggling, and taught you some life-changing lessons that have helped you through your highs and lows. You can draw from these stories as a communication tool to help build your brand.

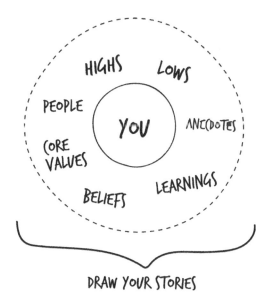

DRAW YOUR STORIES

Without changing your conditioning, you will keep narrating the same way. I hope that you understand the importance of storytelling and are charged to put your story on a page. It will give you insights like never before. This new view will have an impact on how you plan your future. It's not easy to adjust to a new way of thinking. Your old habits and conditioning may be telling you to go back to what was familiar and comfortable, even though you don't want to. If you struggle in any way to maintain the new thinking, let me know, and I can offer you support.

Storytelling is a long-established form of art that has a place in every culture and strata of society going beyond dialect, salient heritage, and native lands. Stories help solidify abstract ideas and diminish the complexity of messages. Therefore, on any occasion, you may come across a question such as "What is your life story?" and realize you can draw inspiration from this book. That would be a gratifying moment for me.

To illustrate, imagine your life ten years from now and work backward. How do you picture your future? What will be your future forward story, and how will you hold it with clarity while having the courage and conviction?

I hope you define your tomorrow through successful anecdotes and work towards that story while holding micro patience and commanding micro speed.

CHAPTER SIX: AUTHENTIC NETWORKING AND RELATIONSHIP BUILDING

"Shweta, my plate is already full. I have no time to waste networking and reaching out to people. I feel buried just trying to catch up on things. I am acing my job and feel stuck in my career. I don't have the time. I don't see the value of having a chat if it's not pointed towards the definitive work I have undertaken."

These are common feedback blurbs I hear from people I coach. Well, the bad news is that if you are acing your job, it's table stakes - it is an expectation. Being really good at your job may not be enough to help you achieve your goals.

The good news is that authentic networking and building your network are crucial not only to your professional success but also to your personal life. Consider it as going to a professional school and reflecting on the invaluable lessons you learn. You will learn things beyond your imagination, which, in turn, will make your life more fulfilling. You build life-long friendships that go well beyond work. It's all about the choices you make. Rather than staying stuck and surrounding yourself with busyness, you will evolve in your RAINBOW journey to reach the pot of gold of your hopes and dreams. This chapter will have a simple but pragmatic framework of the why, what, and how of networking. I hope you use this as an investment process in your life's journey.

As I got busy in my life, similar to most of us, it was getting hard to meet old pals over a coffee chat or dinner to catch up. Deliberately, being extremely intentional, my decade-old friend Sam (who started initially as a colleague) made plans to meet up for dinner one night. It was a ninety-minute drive for each of us, but we were committed to reigniting the good old days. There is no substitute for an in-person meeting. The energy, bonding, camaraderie, love, solidarity, everything about a human connection is priceless and irreplaceable. I missed it sorely and was again reminded during the time of the pandemic of all the basic things we take for granted. Just how the rest of the world deeply felt during the COVID pandemic, although there is some normalcy coming back, it's not the same as before.

As we conversed over a glass of spicy jalapeño margarita, we reminisced about the good times and talked about what had transpired over the years when we couldn't meet up. So much has changed in life, and all those precious experiences he shared were priceless. He worked as a software engineer for a successful financial company in Chicago and was doing pretty well for a few years, but then felt his growth becoming stagnant. He was working away but not getting any developmental opportunities and was getting frustrated. Even more frustrating was when he saw some of his colleagues getting those opportunities. I could relate to the sentiment, having been there myself several times. Well, being frustrated doesn't help, it only makes things worse.

Luckily, my friend decided to invest in an external career

coach to help him through his journey. That investment, in his words, was paid off by leaps and bounds. As they say, don't be penny-wise, pound-foolish. I've been there myself, so I can attest to this. As Sam started his coaching sessions, he clearly realized his blind spots. It was hard to digest them at first, but eventually he realized what he needed to do in addition to being stellar at his job. Doing a good job is the minimal expectation, but a lot more is required to accelerate your development and growth in life. The key lesson Sam shared from his coaching gig was investing time in building relationships based on mutual trust. His mindset changed from a transactional to a trusted one in relationships.

Connecting with other people and building a sense of community within a few groups can give you support. Remember, many people in influential roles from diverse backgrounds have gone through similar challenges in their lives and are willing to help you. Identify people who can be allies in the work you are doing. You cannot do it by yourself. Find people who will elevate you. Having the right people around you at the right time works wonders, and then, of course, your hard work and perseverance towards turning that idea into reality. There are circles of influence and chains of energy cohorts. If someone similar to you can accomplish something in whatever dimension or task you choose to emulate, the prospect of achieving that rises in your own estimation. It gives you hope. Building that network and support system is of paramount importance. Listening to Sam's story resonated with me. This is an essential step in this part of your journey. Take the help - invest in genuine, authentic relationships grounded in mutual trust and respect.

Many of us think we are great at networking, yet we struggle in our careers. I can guarantee breaking most of your myths related to networking as you stay with me in this step of your RAINBOW process.

On a sheet of paper or in your journal, list the people you think you are networking with. Jot down the reasons why you chose those people. Now let's pivot to the why, what, and how of networking, and we will soon come back to your list from above.

Why is Networking Important? What is Your Primary Motivation?

There are two key driving factors behind networking. One is centered around short-term benefits with a myopic view—a short life span. The other is focused on long-term play and forming long-lasting relationships and friendships, which lead to a fulfilling life. It's based on mutual trust and giving in more to the relationship with no expectations. When you are surrounded by meaningful relationships built on trust, your outlook towards life changes, and you find purpose, making your life meaningful.

Narrative changes everything. Focus on building the right one with the long-term lens. Think of Winston Churchill, who, at the height of the Blitz when World War II was about to be lost, urged Londoners to "Keep calm and carry on." Five words, a simple narrative reset that changed the course of history. But of course, not any five words will do. The secret is identifying the ideas that trigger a narrative reset, getting your brain out of a negative spiral and into a productive mindset.

Now, let's go back and resurface your leadership journey— the future version of it.

Think about your career goals, what you outlined in your leadership story from the exercise you completed in the chapter "Storytelling: Offer Your Unique Story," and what help you need to achieve your aspirations. Do you have the necessary network to assist you in achieving your goal or do you need to expand your network? Evidently, there is a clear tie between your career aspirations and your network. Do not underestimate the available resources, and never undermine what they can do for your life. More than seventy percent of jobs are found through networking.

Think Through the Following Questions

- What resources do you need to accomplish what you want?
- What kind of people have the resources?
- How do you cultivate those relationships?
- How do you improve the network you already have?

Jot Down Your Primary Reasons for Networking:

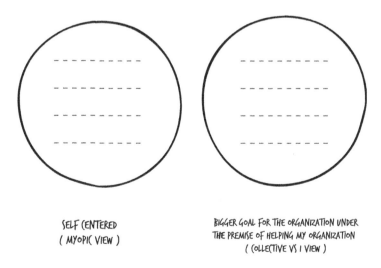

SELF CENTERED
(MYOPIC VIEW)

BIGGER GOAL FOR THE ORGANIZATION UNDER
THE PREMISE OF HELPING MY ORGANIZATION
(COLLECTIVE VS I VIEW)

What You Need to Do

List people in the following circle. Don't overstress, just list the names that come to you. You will likely see a few blanks. There is nothing to worry about, as that is why this exercise is essential. Get grounded in your current landscape and work on aligning with your future leadership story.

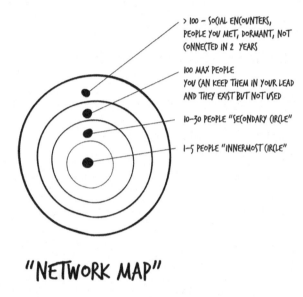

> 100 - SOCIAL ENCOUNTERS, PEOPLE YOU MET, DORMANT, NOT CONNECTED IN 2 YEARS

100 MAX PEOPLE YOU CAN KEEP THEM IN YOUR LEAD AND THEY EXIST BUT NOT USED

10-30 PEOPLE "SECONDARY CIRCLE"

1-5 PEOPLE "INNERMOST CIRCLE"

"NETWORK MAP"

Choose your close circle carefully. Handpick people. Conversations and experiences become perspectives.

There are Three Primary Types of Networks

Internal Network:

- Centric within your organization
- Required to get work done effectively
- Improves your and your team's engagement

External Network:

- It comprises personal and professional networks—people you meet through social and professional engagement.
- Must-have for management roles.
- It is current and future-oriented.
- Helps develop professional skills through coaching and mentoring.
- It exposes you to novelty.

Internal and External Networks:

- Is future-oriented: helps figure out future possibilities, priorities, and challenges.
- It helps you become a more strategic and well-rounded person.
- Instrumental in longer-term career planning or discovering avenues that could lead to a significant career change.

To succeed, you need all three types of networks, but to master internal and external networking, you must interact with people who can open your eyes to new opportunities and help you capitalize on them.

Networking is real work and is at the heart of leadership roles. Invest in relationships.

As you are building these networks, consider downward networking. Research has shown that people who network downward in their organizations have additional leverage. It helps you with intel on trends, the internal and external landscape, and gaining perspective on the ecosystem.

List Your Network Contacts in Three Categories

- Internal Network: getting the job done effectively.
- External Network: discuss important work matters; you confide in evaluating opportunities and discussing critical topics.
- Internal and external networks: people who have made the most significant contributions to your professional development and career advancement.

Identify the network in which you have the most room to expand and grow.

How to Start Building Your Network

- Every month, introduce yourself to one new person.
- Reach out to the dormant person in your network map and connect with that person. Each month, pick one person from that list.
- Identify who you can connect with for internal networking in your current company.
- When you travel for work, make it a point to network meaningfully.
- Connecting with people from various aspects of your

life – college, work, kids' sports team, personal, etcetera – keeps the novelty alive.

- In crowds, parties, etcetera, ask questions. Think of who you want to cultivate a relationship with. It makes people feel important.
- Put in a conscious effort (calendar it)
- Continue to renew your network. Think about a Christmas tree. It needs to be re-lit if one light does not work correctly. Similarly, your network needs to be reconnected frequently.
- Surround yourself with friends and people who offer different points of view, strengths, and abilities. Ask. Listen. Learn.

Always Give

Think about what you can give: what can you do for this person? Always be grateful for having the lens of, "without this person, I would not be the same professional." The reality is that people like people who produce good things for them. Being considerate is always associated and linked with greater happiness that goes beyond materialistic and otherworldly power. People with an accommodating and beneficial nature, incredible positive character, and an educational nature facilitate a successful career for themselves. Their kindness and benevolence are conducive to a desirable future.

Pay it Forward

Everyone has time to pay it forward. Make the time. It helps others and feels great.

As you progress through this, remember trust is an essential factor in life. It is an invaluable and permanent asset. Building trust with people you work with is necessary.

Now you understand the critical role networking and building trusted partnerships play in your life. Start being tactical, put an immediate plan together, and implement it. After you have placed names in this framework, it is time to start executing to build your network. Calendar it. Hanging out with your list only prolongs your unhappiness and perpetuates the dismay in your life. It's time to take the next step.

CHAPTER SEVEN: LISTENING TO INTUITION

"An intuitive mind is a sacred gift, and the rational mind is a faithful servant. We have created a society that honors the servant and has forgotten the gift."
~ Albert Einstein

I'm often asked, "Did you make an important decision about your life just because you trusted your gut?" and my answer is, "Yes." I simply followed my instincts. In this chapter, through sharing stories and the key elements of how you can nurture your intuition, you will be able to believe in the power of intuition and, more importantly, commit to putting that into practice. It gets better only when you start building that muscle. In order for its magic to happen, it would help if you believed in it. This is not science - this is how you train your brain and heart to get in sync, creating a feeling within your body that only you experience. Our intuition is so deeply instinctual that even if we've been out of touch with it for our entire lives, it's still there inside us, waiting for us to summon its wisdom. As it's so personal to you, no one can guide you better in any given situation. You make the right call alone. Because of this, trusting your intuition is the ultimate act of trusting yourself.

Always Trust Your Gut

It was a cold, snowy day in February in beautiful Wisconsin. I was pregnant with my second child, and right after the Packers won the Super Bowl, we had to rush to the hospital. After completing all the formalities, I was admitted to the hospital, patiently waiting for my little bundle of joy. It was a big hospital with hundreds of cookie-cutter rooms. While I was having severe contractions, I felt that my daughter, then five years old, was born in the same room. We knew it was the same hospital but the same room- what were the odds? One in a million, maybe. I shared this hunch with my husband, Mike, and he almost chuckled. He thought his wife had started hallucinating amidst severe pain.

Nonetheless, I insisted. It wasn't as if he had a choice. You take orders when your wife is in labor - logic doesn't necessarily work. He went to the front desk, seeking an answer. Technology and all the systems weren't perfect those days, and it required some manual effort to pull the paper trail as we were trying to retrieve five-year-old information. My husband returned to the room, grinning from ear to ear, much to my delight. This was right when I was in the middle of getting an epidural. The pain was brutal. Seeing my affliction, my husband couldn't keep the suspense anymore. He said, "Yes, our daughter was born in this room five years ago. How in the world did you get this feeling?"

The pain subsided instantaneously as the feelings of a proud mother's intuition took over; this feeling was a lot stronger than the pain I was going through, at least in that moment. Both my children, five years apart, were born in the same room. It's a story meant for the grandchildren. This instance inspired me to put more trust and belief into my intuition. In the beginning, what started as a hunch and curiosity has grown into professional strength, life skills, and passion I'm always looking to improve on.

I would never have found out about this had I not listened to my intuition.

When Someone Projects Their True Self Onto You

My boss landed a fantastic gig outside of the organization, which resulted in some restructuring in my department. As a result of this restructuring, I had a new boss: Pat. It was an interesting, short-term relationship. He had an intimidating personality, which was okay. However, he was set in his ways and was not open to listening to others. My kids were little then, and my schedule included dropping them off at daycare in the morning. We were trying to schedule a weekly meeting, and he said, "The only time that works for me is seven to eight in the morning."

I said, "That might be hard given my daycare drop-off schedule."

He responded, "It's your issue to figure out your personal life."

It was a pretty stressful situation. I was in the early management phase and did not have any sponsors or champions in the organization. The few interactions I had with him made me so uncomfortable to the extent that I was prepared for the worst possible outcome. Something in my heart was telling me that I needed to move on. I started exploring other options only two weeks after being under his leadership. Thankfully, I received positive responses. I had not realized until then that I had unintentionally and unknowingly built a little brand for myself. This was helping me. I officially reported to Pat for six weeks. It was the shortest ever stint in my career. Later, after I was out of his conserve, I learned that he was biased and treated women poorly. That was his reputation and brand, which I was unaware of at that time. However, I listened to my heart, and it did not feel right for me to stick with him any longer than absolutely necessary.

Listen to your heart. Your inner voice has the answer.

Trusting My Intuition Helped Someone Recover from a Performance Plan

I was newly appointed in a supervisory role. Along with the usual responsibilities, I inherited an employee who wasn't performing and was consequently put on a performance plan. Let's call her Trish. Trish's perception wasn't good, and she struggled with performance issues for almost a year. After meeting her a few times, something did not seem right. She was in the trenches knowing that she might not have a job in ninety days. Being a single mom of two daughters, this was a daunting thought for her. At the same time, she was going through her divorce process. How would she survive?

It seemed like she was not the type of person who needed to be on a plan. My gut was telling me to dig deeper, so I did. I had several conversations with all the stakeholders and got a better perspective on her previous roles, past performances, challenges, strengths, etcetera. I got a 360-degree view of her. Furthermore,

I had some healthy debates with my manager on this, as she thought I was wasting my time and wouldn't be able to help Trish recover from her situation. I didn't have to make any effort to dig deeper – the given direction was for her to exit as she was perceived as being a poor performer. However, I listened to my gut and dug even deeper. She and I worked on 30, 60, and 90-day plans together to get her back. We had clearly established priorities, planned actions, and check-ins to meet and track her progress. Through this process, I realized that Trish was the victim of imposter syndrome. It took an effort to overcome this, but imagine how much worse this would have been if she had lost her job. She not only came out of her situation, but came out with flying colors. She needed the boost, the kick, and the belief that she could do this. This moment was most gratifying for me as my heart had guided me to look into this further and believe in Trish, not what was said and perceived to be accurate.

Intuition led, followed by the heart - the recipe for a fulfilling life.

We all have intuition. It's our choice to listen to it. The best decisions I have made in life have been intuition-led. The data was sometimes neither enough nor compelling, and in some cases, completely opposite of the norm. I was listening to my body's reaction and the thoughts that whispered into my ears when making those decisions.

Things That You Will Need to Overcome to Grow Your Intuition

Overthinking

We as human beings are hard-wired to overthink most situations. The definition of intuition is "the ability to understand something instinctively, without the need for conscious reasoning." By the definition of intuition, you have to put a pause on overthinking. If you don't intentionally put effort into ignoring it, overthinking will continue to be one of your biggest barriers. Putting excessive and unnecessary thought into every decision and walking through the countless scenarios and outcomes can lead you away from your gut instinct, especially when you're overthinking to rationalize something. In these cases, you are not allowing your thought process to flow freely or organically because it is following a specific protocol to build a case for something you've already made up your mind on. Let your thoughts flow freely, allowing you to be in touch with your natural instinct. Magic will follow by itself. Normalize not overthinking.

Slowing Down to Speed Up

You might have a zillion things going on at the same time. If you don't take a moment to relax your mind and manage it carefully, it slows you down in recognizing and processing the information you receive, not only in your mind but also in your body. To enable this, you must mentally and physically clear away the clutter. It may look like learning to say "NO" to make room for yourself in real life situations. It could also mean stepping away from a situation to gain further clarity. Steve Jobs was known for taking long walks when he was stuck on a problem to gain a moment of true clarity. When you step away from any situation, you give yourself permission to slow down and see things from a different perspective. That clarity is like a fresh breath of air: pure inspiration. This intentionality provides space for your intuition to grow.

Some Key Elements to Help You Nurture Your Intuition

- Close the door, turn off all distracting electronic devices, and take a few deep, slow breaths to relax your body.
- Be attentive to what's going on around you.
- Listen, more than you speak.
- "Quiet time," or "me time," is one of the most valuable investments you'll ever make.
- Choose your circle of friends, acquaintances, and coworkers carefully.
- Believing in your heart and keeping your faith.
- Recognizing the importance of playing the long-term game rather than focusing on short-term pleasures.
- It's okay to deal with short-term discomfort for the long-term future.
- Listen to your voice – speak out loud to yourself.
- Journaling: get it all out there. It provides the clarity needed at every juncture.
- Leave your comfort zone frequently to avoid getting trapped in your "basic survival mode."
- When you give yourself permission without an iota of doubt, all the forces in the universe will align to make it happen. Magic follows.
- With purposeful practice and frequent use, your intuition will become more powerful and better serve its purpose,

guiding you home to yourself.

Never lose sight of the choices you have in your life; it can be liberating when you recognize your options and make decisions based on what's right for you. Let your intuition freely inject itself into you and help guide you through your beautiful life journey. More than anything else, you will learn about yourself.

Some choices will be risky, but extraordinary lives and careers involve risks.

CHAPTER EIGHT: RESILIENCE, ADAPTING TO CHANGE AND PERSEVERANCE

When Darwin proposed his evolutionary theory of "SURVIVAL OF THE FITTEST," he described the mechanism of natural selection. The term "fittest" is often misinterpreted as the quickest, most clever, and most potent. Instead, he referred to the "fittest" as the population most capable of adapting to changes in their environment. The ability to persevere through challenges and adapt to change are essential skills that will help you learn and thrive in your career now and in the future. Both skills are closely related to one unifying factor – mindset. In this chapter, I hope you will realize that one of the most significant competencies you will need is the resiliency muscle. To reach your personal and professional goals and live a fulfilled life, you need to be able to change direction quickly in a world that is constantly changing and moving.

Life can throw you curveballs. Uncertainty and unrest from changes at work, discomfort when feeling disliked by a colleague, etc. What does it take to be okay on the inside no matter what is happening in the outside world? Life is easy when things are going your way, but what truly defines your character is how you react when things go south. You are truly put to the test when faced with the impossible. Remember, when almost everything is uncertain, anything is possible. You can open doors you may never have seen otherwise by stepping into fear and taking chances. Character trumps everything - it's what defines us at our core.

It is hoped things will all go according to plan, but they seldom do. Getting frustrated or cursing your luck isn't helpful. Fighting this is like fighting against gravity—good luck with that. No one has ever won a fight like that. A better approach is to expect change to be the norm and give yourself permission to be positively surprised when things work. Other times, take it in stride and find the silver lining. The trick is to look past the situation and acknowledge how it can bring you rewards and opportunities. Don't let what's happening around you get to you and weigh you down.

There Was Only One of Me in the Room

As I took on a new area of responsibility as a technology director, I recall my first meeting with business partners. Upon entering the rectangular, crowded conference room, I noticed that I was the only female in there. The space was occupied almost entirely by roughly forty men. People were still trickling in, and soon we had a room filled with around fifty men and only one woman – me. It was a freak show. I noticed it vividly as I was new to my role and wanted to understand the landscape. To put it all out there, I had near-paralyzing fear and nervousness. I was intimidated and thought I had lost my voice — it was tough being the only one of my kind (female) in the room. I barely managed to introduce myself when my turn came. I pondered whether it was the proper role I'd signed up for. Did I want to do this? Did I want to get this "Imposter Syndrome" feeling every time I hung out with the "men's group?" My dad's voice whispered in my ears, "Just one more step"—I decided to pursue it with all my heart. My first step was to get those demons out of my head. So what if I was the only female in the room? So what if I was new to the role? So what if I had to fit in and stand out later? All of these life experiences were meant only to exercise my adaptability muscle. I was preparing for the future.

I had to internalize that this was normal for a new job, and I was doing just fine - that helped my nerves. I felt less anxious and more present and focused on the work, which led to me thinking less about who was in the room and more about what I needed to do. I was entering a more positive cycle that reinforced itself; when I focused on the good, the good around me increased.

In hindsight, it was a terrific experience for me because I learned a lot. Since then, I have been in many similar situations. Everything improved from how I felt the first time, what I learned, and the perspective I gained from subsequent times in similar circumstances. I learned how to deal with being pushed out of my comfort zone; I can't change the way things are, but I can change my perspective and look at these situations through a positive lens. The fundamental learning was that change is inevitable, and the more resilient I become, the better off I will be. It is crucial to persevere and change in order to see it from the right lens.

This one is for all the amazing women out there. Your "female" traits make you a great leader. For the most part, women are still primarily responsible for raising their families. It's a part of your genetic structure. That means you take responsibility for nurturing people to feel included and valued. You have a natural, healthy sense of doubt and a more profound sense of intuition. You often meet with other women and talk about whether you could be doing things better, whether you are doing enough. Every night, when I lie in bed, I list the things I did that day, and what I could have done better. At times, I can't even remember the things I did well. Don't you go through similar notions? We are self-punitive and have the grit to keep pushing, keep pushing, keep pushing.

Change is your only "constant" in life, and your resilience is your greatest strength.

FOCUS is the Recipe

In his quadrennial period of engineering college, my husband, Mayank, was counted as a backbencher whose class notes would just be a quarter of a page of tiny scrawls scribbled.

He would usually play cricket or pull an all-nighter of three card poker sessions with friends in the dorm. Clearly, it did not seem like a recipe for academic success by any stretch.

Surprisingly, he aced his exams; everyone, including the professors, were shocked. Students who pulled all-nighters studying didn't do as well as he did. He later was picked by a good company through campus recruiting, landing him a good job.

How is This Explained?

A few years ago, I would have answered "Genius." I now think the true answer is "focus." His notes were brief because he could focus, absorb, ingest, and synthesize the key points. Although he didn't work hard, he worked smart and had fun while excelling by prioritizing the right things with impeccable focus.

I believe that focus, more than intellect, is the real game-changer in life. I have experienced this myself. The results were insignificant when I spent my early years in the corporate world daydreaming and distracted. However, once I had a wake-up call and got into an intense focus mode, I could see how my learning and development instantaneously accelerated.

We like to simplify things by using labels such as "stupid" and "smart." I can trace all the ups and downs in my life to just my level of focus.

Prioritize, optimize, focus. We all have talent inside, but without focus, it remains inconspicuous. Give your genius a chance to flourish. "Hidden genius" is no genius.

The Biggest Obstacle, as It Turns Out, is Always Inside Your Head

My neighbor-turned-friend, VK, lived a few houses down from me. We would often take walks in the evenings and talk about his plan to quit his fantastic job at a top Fortune 100 company and pursue an MBA from a great business school. The plan sounded crazy—nobody I knew had done that. When you come from a small town like Lucknow, it all sounds like a farfetched pipe dream. Yet, VK made it to the University of Chicago. When that happened my "pipe dream" suddenly became within reach. Essentially, VK did the hard part of figuring things out and creating the path, I just walked on it. I sometimes wonder, what if I hadn't met him?

I may have imagined that everything on my bucket list was hard, maybe even undoable. When you assume that something is impossible, sometimes it is just that you haven't met the person who has already done it. Whenever your mind says, "I can't do this," challenge it. It is probably just an assumption. You can do a lot more than you think you can.

"Whether you think you can, or you think you can't, you're right."
~Henry Ford

A Story of Perseverance

My dear friend Simran authors this story. It is her life story.

My story is full of unexpected twists and turns across all critical junctures of my professional and personal life; some would say my journey to where I am today is a pure miracle and others would say it's the result of perseverance. I was born in India when a girl child was not welcomed with joy in some parts of the country. I grew up with my grandparents, far from my parents and siblings. Given the poverty and lack of opportunities I experienced, it was crystal clear to me at a very early age that education would be my equalizer for opportunities in life. I was lucky enough to be enrolled in a school, but it didn't have a lot of resources or optimal infrastructure.

I had to be innovative to supplement my limited academic learnings with broader skills to ensure my education was well-rounded. I would wake up before the crack of dawn to diligently read the newspaper lying on our neighbors' doorstep, sneak into the library at every possible opportunity to read books from numerous genres (spiritual, teenage fiction, science). My ears would perk up when the television channel was turned to current affairs and quiz shows. I had always dreamt of pursuing higher education and joining the corporate world. However, higher studies came with a hefty price tag. I mustered the courage to become vulnerable, and I was fortunate to find a sponsor willing to fund my education.

I pursued an MBA in Finance from one of the top B-schools in India. The two years of B-school exposed me to the brightest minds in India, and I could envision the meaning of "The world is your oyster." My non-traditional resume and experiences caught recruiters' attention during campus placements, and a Top 10 Fortune company shortlisted me for their prestigious leadership program. During my interview, I was very candid with the panel, which comprised the CFO and head of HR, about my life struggles and poverty that helped me acquire life skills like a survival instinct, an eye for opportunity, and how to stretch a dollar past its breaking point. I demonstrated that these skills could be a vital business asset. One should never undermine the power of authenticity. I was presented with the opportunity to join the prestigious program and lead a finance function for a struggling business unit as my first job. I met my husband on the program, and we both pursued this journey together while having a long-distance marriage.

After graduating from one of the most prestigious business schools, I was eager to use my leadership skills to solve real-time business problems. I was presented an opportunity to join a business as their CFO, partnering with the CEO to lead its turnaround. I doubted my readiness for the job, but my mentors could see more in me than I could and took a chance on me. Little did I know the CEO would soon leave the company, and I would be leading the turnaround. This role was one of the most challenging and rewarding experiences of my life. It taught me many things that I can now use in my professional and personal lives.

My journey has taught me a few key lessons. People are the most valued asset of an organization. The key is to take chances on people; they will surprise you. Growth happens during uncomfortable times. Take risks, and learn to fail fast. Persevere!

The time-old adage is so true that time flies when one has fun. It's been fifteen years in the corporate world for me. I wake up every day as excited as I was on the first day of the job, and if it were not for the authentic relationships with the people around me, I would not have been able to turn my dream into reality.

Anti-Social Person Having a Successful Social Network Channel

"I don't want to hang out with people. I don't want to step outside the home. You guys go ahead. I am fine the way I am. I don't enjoy other people's company." This was my sister growing up.

This type of personality probably contributed to, "I don't want to ever get married and leave the comfort of my home."

Growing up, we had to negotiate with her to attend a select few social events, birthday parties, etcetera, which were by no means pleasant conversations inside our home.

Everyone is different, and you must respect their opinions and choices. It's their life after all. Three siblings, five years apart, wired completely differently, with different perspectives on what they wanted to do—a typical family story.

Fast-forward, as they say, you never stop growing and changing. My sister had a son who inspired her to step outside her comfort zone little by little over the years. Because of that, the same person has evolved from being anti-social to someone who started a successful YouTube channel that rapidly grew one year ago. Also she recently celebrated twenty-one years of successful wedlock. As I reflect, there are lots of lessons in her story.

As people on our own journey, we become different people throughout our lives. The key is to be open to anything life brings our way and embrace it with an open heart. Miracles happen.

Any Moment Can be a Turning Point in Life

My brother's entire focus as a child was on food; that was where it started and exactly where it ended. Food was all he could think of, from breakfast to lunch to dinner. I would describe my brother as a food devotee growing up. Since that was the sole purpose of his existence—at least it seemed like that—I saw no hope in his future whatsoever. I thought with this attitude in life, he would barely make ends meet.

I nor anyone else saw any ray of light in him. The credit goes to his relentless focus on food. A sudden change happened to him as he was in his last year of high school. To our sudden (yet pleasant) surprise, he got admitted into a pretty good engineering college. When he broke this news to me, I thought he was just kidding and didn't believe it until I saw the acceptance letter. I thought he managed to get into a decent undergraduate college, but he again surprised me when he called saying he got accepted to Purdue for his MBA. I simply had no words.

What Could Have Potentially Elucidated This?

A few years ago, I would have said genius combined with luck, but now, I think the honest answer is a lack of awareness of available options. There came a time in his life when my brother had to pick a lane, and he picked engineering. After completing his undergrad degree and becoming a professional in that field for several years, he realized that wasn't something he wanted to pursue for the rest of his life. He decided to pursue an MBA, but only from a reputable college. For someone I saw no hope in growing up, I could not be more proud to watch his accomplishments.

We all have talents hidden within us, and at times when we lack awareness, followed by focus and relentless perseverance, they never come out. Give your genius a chance to flourish.

I Changed My Job Every Eighteen to Twenty-Four Months without Leaving My Company

Leonard Sweet once said, "Stagnation is death. If you don't change, you die. It's that simple. It's that scary."

I was in my first corporate job for a good couple years, to the point where I could do the job in my sleep. It made me complacent, which wasn't the best for my learning and development. Out of sheer chance and luck, I had the privilege of meeting one of the most influential people in my life, and a brief hallway conversation with him lit up the kindle in me, for which I am forever grateful. At times, you meet people who change your perspective and life forever—this was one of those remarkable moments for me. Without meeting this amazing person, Rob, I wouldn't be the person I am today neither personally nor professionally.

He said, "I've heard about you and wanted to reach out. Glad we ran into each other." I was clueless as to why he said that. We formally met in the upcoming week, and he offered me a job in an area I had no experience in. He said, "I trust you will do great; just don't mess up big." That instilled unwavering confidence and self-belief in me. Since then, I have changed my role every eighteen to twenty-four months in some shape or form, attributed to the experience I had with Rob. I moved from business areas where I was extremely comfortable into entirely new areas with new responsibilities. It seemed like I was barely going to survive for the first several months. However, it was critical to learn new areas of expertise in the changing world so I wouldn't lose my options. I realized that I would lose more than just my skills if I weren't using and upping my skills. I would lose future choices.

Despite all the compelling forces pushing towards states of acceptance and moving on, it is considerably harder to let go of the past. However, it was necessary for me to keep moving and evolving so I could write about my future rather than have someone else write it for me. Recognizing and practicing the "No Regret Policy," I had a choice to make. My past was great, but the future could always be better. I chose the future every single time.

A Tough Business Partner: A Story of Perseverance

A while back, I found myself in a challenging position where my business partner, Gordon, was bringing out the worst in me. Gordon was one level higher than me. Though he was pretty good at running his area, he wasn't open to outsiders. Yes, I was an outsider within the same company. He was one of the critical stakeholders I needed to align with for everything I was leading. It was exhausting to figure out a plan, align the strategy, secure funding, and execute that plan. It was hard to deal with it every single day. It wasn't only hard for me, it was also hard for my colleagues and teams. The atmosphere this gentleman created was tyrannical. Imagine going to work every day and being in meetings where you are under the impression you can't have an opinion, let alone share it. If you were gutsy and shared your opinion (which I did a few times), God forbid, you got pin-drop silence and perhaps a few stares. Despite how miserable it was, I was somehow hell-bent on gaining his trust. I wasn't willing to give up on this, at least not yet.

Harvard Business School professor Noam Wasserman, who published the book "The Founder's Dilemmas", discovered that sixty-five percent of startups failed because of the co-founder conflict. Imagine the micro and macro failures that regularly occur in the corporate world due to this.

Why couldn't we stand in the same line and go hand in hand? Was that because we didn't have the same core values and overarching goals for the business, or did we not have trust in each other, for whatever reason? I wanted to have a frank, comprehensive discussion with Gordon to agree on the code of behavior and unify the understanding of our business's visions, needs, goals, and expectations. I wanted to discuss with him the possibilities of setting up mutual respect between us and what I could do to attain that goal of building our partnership. It would be a heart-to-heart talk, and I hoped to reignite the flames within him towards making decisions together.

I resorted to seeking some common ground with him while reserving my differences. I took the first step of sending him an email requesting a meeting. There were many steps after that in an attempt to build that partnership. As I entered his office for our first meeting, my heart sank, anticipating the worst-case scenario. I experienced a myriad of feelings – hope, fear, anxiety, joy, annoyance, etcetera. Nevertheless, it had to start somewhere. I gathered all the courage in the world, took a leap, and expressed my concerns related to the lack of what appeared to be a shared vision, strategy, and camaraderie among the teams and the impact this was having on the team as a whole. I was modest in listening to him, his pain points, suggestions, and opinions with an open mind. His concerns were centered around suboptimal processes, slow and bureaucratic innovation, and funding challenges. As I listened to him with a calm, open mind, I realized some of his concerns were legitimate, and I needed to do more of an education session with him so he could see what we were doing to address those concerns. These were not new concerns, and we had been intentionally working towards a plan. He just wasn't aware or kept informed. More listening and less talking. It was one of the hundreds of conversations we had – almost twice a week. Some were painful, some not so much. I didn't think I was making much progress until my boss told me in the annual performance review that Gordon gave some great feedback about me. Gordon appreciated my first step in having the conversation and understanding his point of view. He also appreciated that I wouldn't give up and was persistent in solving the issues. He valued my partnership. I was pleasantly surprised, as this was the last thing I had expected to hear. I realized that not giving up and persevering through things could help. In this case, it only took two years.

Don't give up on your dreams a minute earlier than you need to. You might be a step away from a literal miracle.

Stop assuming, speak up. Often, we don't speak up because of the fear of facing rejection. Giving significant consideration to what others will decide or say is the most impolite thing we can do to ourselves. Speak up and talk to others. It is better to listen to a no than believe in a potential no.

I Am Not Good Enough

I get extremely disheartened when I hear my cousin feel this deep within herself. She does not verbalize it, making it harder on me and even harder on her. I honestly don't understand the "Why?" behind this feeling.

For as long as I can remember, Simona has been an inspiration and strength to me in her ways. She is full of energy, positivity, love, warmth, and living life as it comes - she probably doesn't even realize it. She is the epitome of love and empathy, which I believe should be among the most preserved traits among the busy world we live in. Titles or bank balances should not measure people's success; they should be measured by how they make others around them feel.

I was dealing with a significant personal issue related to my teenage daughter, and the first person I wanted to talk it out with was her. She listened, empathized, and gave me pragmatic advice. She took me down memory lane and reminded me of our teenage years growing up and how mentally, emotionally, socially, and physically challenging those days were. It made me understand that my daughter was going through a similar phase, trying to discover herself and build her identity. She needed a certain amount of autonomy and room to stretch, take risks, try new things, and grow. Simona reached out to my daughter as someone she could talk to. Things settled down ever since they were both able to connect. I don't think anyone else would have done this the way she did.

For whom does Simona believe she is not good enough? Aren't we our own prisoners?

A Few Lessons

- Stop thinking you are not good enough because you are great enough. The buck stops with you—you need to believe in yourself.
- Be kind. It's not that hard.
- The "What" is important in life, but the "How" is even more important.
- To be successful and achieve your goals, focus on your strengths versus your opportunities. Your strengths will help you craft your unwritten life story.

Persevere in the Moment, Despite the Hardships

My friend Michael works for a large organization. He was involved in a complex situation that required him to evaluate an issue that entailed a multimillion-dollar deal and complex technology implementation for a large customer carefully and within a short timeframe. Michael had to quickly gather years of data in just four days to help his company's most important customer.

Michael's company had an important customer in its portfolio. They generated tens of millions of dollars yearly in revenue from implementing massive initiatives at a large financial company. One of the initiatives involved a large technology implementation to replace the current complex and expensive legacy systems. The other initiative was the management of agents across the globe, which was a more than eight-year-old legacy maintenance initiative.

The customer leaders, including the Chief Technology Officer and his directors, expressed serious concerns over the ongoing implementation initiatives due to perceived suboptimal results and alluded to discontinuing the contract, which was up for renewal in a month. This occurred one week after Michael joined.

It was a surprise to Michael, as he was new to the customer, it was only in his second week in the role, and he barely had the opportunity to build any trust with the customer leaders or have a good understanding of the landscape. He had to put together a plan to figure out this mess immediately. He promptly reached out to his firm's implementation leaders and understood the current landscape. He reached out to the customer leaders and expressed regret on behalf of his organization and requested they provide an opportunity to revert with a quick postmortem on issues, preventive, and corrective measures. Michael met with customer leaders, including executive directors and the Chief Technology Officer, and understood the key concerns during the first two days. He also met with his globally distributed key employees during those two days. Michael took all of the customer leaders and consultants' point of views into account.

He quickly realized that some of the customers' complaints were out of proportion, and his clairvoyance allowed him to take an unbiased stand.

He realized that the concerns were pretty much aligned across the board. He broadly categorized the customers' problems into a broken delivery process, inadequate technical knowledge, and the delivered output not aligning with business expectations. Further, he determined that those concerns were attributed to several qualitative and quantitative measures. Since the contract was up for renewal shortly, he had to collate more than three years of information and provide the customer with a report within a week.

He analyzed delivered output for the prior one-and-a-half years and the velocity metrics. He learned that some produced work didn't align with the product features, but the features and requirements constantly kept changing and reprioritizing. He realized that customer product managers couldn't finalize key product features.

He then had to quickly plan how to best address the three concerns in order to meet the customer's expectations. He met with the firm's executives and explored deferred payment options. He emphasized that he wanted to go above and beyond and be a thought leader for the customer, not just an implementation partner. He called in a meeting with people from both parties and provided solid plans for improving the situation: a six-month deferred payment option (which was well acknowledged). He also had the customer recognize their problems with constantly changing product requirements.

In this pursuit, he had to obtain assimilated data to put forward and make judgment calls to address the customer's concerns, listen to his conscience, and take an unbiased stand. Michael not only kept working with the customer, but he also set the stage for a more than $9 million modernization project with them.

"The difference between ordinary and extraordinary is that little extra."
– Jimmy Johnson

Never give up; do a little extra.

We all desire to live successful, happy, and fulfilling lives. To achieve what we all desire, we need to be proactive about how we manage the change we face in our lives. Denial and resisting change will only result in you living a miserable life. Therefore, it is crucial to learn how to be adaptable, resilient, and persevere. These three things are key to successfully adapting to the constant impact that change will have on your life. You have the freedom to shape your life. The keys to unlocking this step are right in your hands. Don't be your own prisoner, you owe it to yourself.

Highs and lows are an integral part of our lives. Our ability to be adaptable, resilient, and persevere makes all the difference to our growth. Don't let your downfalls overshadow your successes and dictate your future life choices in both professional and personal aspects. Ups and downs, benefits, and pitfalls are an indispensable part of life. Every now and then, take a moment to evaluate the highs and lows while getting into a rhythm and also having fun.

Celebrate the uphill and downhill battles. Embrace life's highs and lows—even the unavoidable moments of suffering.

UPS AND DOWNS ARE NECESSARY IN LIFE BECAUSE
EVEN IN ECG A STRAIGHT LINE MEANS GAME OVER

CHAPTER NINE: EQ IS FAR MORE IMPORTANT THAN IQ

"I was well on my way to advancing my career, yet I participated in career-derailing behavior."

"I was accelerating on a different tangent more than my EQ could handle. My wit and intelligence fueled my vertical progress, but my emotional intelligence was lagging. I lacked inner adroitness that required my immediate awareness and attention. I wish I had learned this earlier on in my life. It would have saved me many headaches and heartaches," a close friend of mine, Amy, shared.

An IQ test can only take you so far in life. Emotional intelligence is a critical skill she learned a little late in life. However, it provided her with a completely different lens on how to handle situations in her life. She was hitting the glass ceiling in her career, but it wasn't about doing more and trying harder. It was about discovering what she needed to do differently. Unfortunately, it took a toll on her personal life, sadly having a long-term impact.

Emotional intelligence is not talked about considerably enough. It is neither part of the curriculum in schools nor taught anywhere formally. Lower EQ can make or break your life. This chapter will show how oblivious we are to our trigger points and how we use our emotions ineffectively. You will be able to see its impact on people and how it can shut them down. You will have good and bad days, but how do you equip yourself to handle them differently? Step one is recognizing that this muscle is a "must-have" in life, and is gained only by choosing to do something differently. I advise the folks I coach that building emotional intelligence is a long process, and such changes take time, intentionality, dedication, and guidance. Just when we think we've got it, a situation or person comes along that reminds us that demonstrating emotional intelligence is a lifelong learning process that betters your core. Give it time, and let the changes sink in. The gradual improvements throughout the process will help you transcend to another level.

EQ : Under Construction

Managing Emotional Reactions and Developing Stronger Intelligence Skills

My protégé, Ben, is in his mid-forties. Ben is an executive and holds a leadership position at a large insurance company. He was known for his innate ability to solve complex problems. Within the company, he grew through the ranks given his exceptional talent in his areas of technical expertise. Despite his brilliance and competency, he has struggled over the last two years. He may have been struggling prior, but he just recently realized that he was grappling. He shared his daily struggles with his peers, team, business partners, and boss. He thought an imaginary and indestructible wall was created between him and others.

He believed others were conspiring against him and failed to understand why everyone around him behaved the way they did, leaving him completely clueless.

According to Ben, nothing changed – he was still delivering incredible results, sharing his smarts and knowledge at every possible opportunity. He had brilliant ideas to solve complex and challenging problems, yet he felt like the world was against him. Ben shared an instance in which he was in a meeting with forty people. The meeting was related to a high-visibility project with some stringent deadlines. The team was still wrapping up the initial discovery phase and working to create a detailed plan, but Ben was under tremendous pressure. As the meeting was wrapping up, he asked the project manager for a project plan. The project manager was still working on it and said she needed a few weeks to share one. Ben said, "This is your job. You need to have a plan, and it's unacceptable that you don't." He became emotionally overwhelmed while sharing this experience. Mind you, this was in front of forty people as the meeting was wrapping up and people were leaving. I probed to see if Ben thought there was a better way to handle this, and not to my surprise, he still believed that "his way" was the right way to continue to deliver results. He was still persistent and couldn't see through things. It's not about how smart or intelligent you are, it's how you approach situations and exercise your EQ to influence people around you.

He shared another instance in which he mentioned brilliant ideas his company talked about were his ideas five years ago, and how he shared them with the senior leadership over the years. There were a lot of name-callings in the conversation. He shared how he was close to the executives, giving examples of his conversations with the CFO, COO, etc. As he talked to me, I could sense a lot of pride in his words, but I could also catch a glimpse of his ostentatious self, filled with arrogance and narcissism. It was all about Ben – how he continuously portrayed his exceptional smartness and quick wit, that he had the technical chops, he had it all figured out, and how others needed to step up and do their part, etcetera... Blah, blah, blah.

As I heard his stories, it was not hard to see where Ben's issues laid and why he was struggling. He was completely oblivious to his self-absorbed and self-obsessive nature and the impact his behavior had on everyone around him, especially the damage being done to his brand. I told him, "If you become angry and express it right away, either verbally or written, you can't take it back." Give yourself time to think about which approach will be most effective. There's a difference between being right and being wise, and you need to understand that small gray area. You want to speak the truth, but you also want to know how to speak the truth in a way that allows people to hear what you are saying. "Oh, Ben, you've got to use more than just your brainpower to figure out when and how to make yourself heard."

As it turns out, at least in Ben's case, success is a matter of emotion, relationships, and character rather than raw intelligence. It didn't matter how brilliant Ben was. What mattered (and what was missing) was how he could connect, understand, and inspire other people.

Maya Angelou once said, "People will forget what you said, people will forget what you did, but people will never forget how you made them feel." This philosophy certainly holds true in life. EQ plays a crucial role in our daily lives, but the good news is that it can be learned, developed, and refined. There are ways to increase your EQ:

- Being present in the moment.
- Using active listening skills.
- Responding, not reacting, to situations.
- Empathizing with others.

Context is Everything

A few years ago, it was a dark winter evening in Wisconsin. After a long day at work, I walked into my house only to be welcomed by complete pin-drop silence, which was unusual. I soon realized that my in-laws (visiting us from India), my six-year-old son, and my eleven-year-old daughter were sitting at the dining table with a pout. I was puzzled about what was going on – all four were seated with a fascinating, confused, angry look. I asked, "So, how was everyone's day?" It seemed like they were waiting for that very moment to burst. My mother-in-law exclaimed, "These kids have no manners or etiquette whatsoever on how to talk to the elderly." She had barely finished saying that as my eleven-year-old daughter interrupted and complained, "Dadi and Dadu (grandma and grandpa) were teaching us not so good words." There in my head, I was trying to put the two and two together and could barely wait to hear more. The grandparents and grandkids, who had bonded so well, were suddenly on each other's cases. As a part of our routine, the grandparents usually taught and quizzed the kids on math, English, etcetera. That day, they had quizzed the kids on opposites – tall-short, big-small, dirty-clean, male dog – female dog, except for female dog they used the name that can be interpreted as a swear word. The kids freaked out. They weren't supposed to say the opposite out loud for the last one! They ultimately lost it. Rightfully so. They informed their grandparents that you are out of line and intend to teach us this, that you are obscure and inappropriate, and so

97

on. Hearing this, my in-laws freaked out, as being called "mean" was out of place for them. They could not understand why they were being called that. What did they do wrong?

Context is everything. You miss the whole point of a conversation without having one.

As I heard this, I couldn't help but laugh out loud. The beauty of it all was that no one was wrong. Coming from India, I could relate to what the grandparents were trying to teach and their intent – that's how it was done in India, they knew no better. I could also relate to why my kids were behaving the way they did. To clarify, it's inappropriate to use the word "mean" in Indian culture, just as it is inappropriate to use a dog's opposite gender name in the western part of the world. I explained this context and differences in culture, ways of living, and communication to all of them. In the end, they realized how they completely misunderstood each other as a result of no context.

How often do we misinterpret situations or people without a good understanding of the context in our lives? Plenty of times, at least for me.

Context allows us to respond to situations in a far more effective and mature manner. It's a technique that innovates with your EQ, while continuously strengthening that muscle.

Knowing When to Teach is a More Valuable Skill Than Your Ability to Teach

I've had a deep connection with my nephew, Ivaan (he's only five), since the day he was born, despite only meeting him five times. But who says time spent has anything to do with the feelings and connections we make in our lives? My family and I have weekly FaceTime calls with him and his family. Given that he's the youngest and extremely gullible, we would joke around and make him say or do silly things, all in the spirit of fun. During one of the calls only a few months ago, my dear husband taught Ivaan a lesson on how to do his chores, specifically to clean up when he wraps up playing with his puzzles. He listened and tried to respond with, "My mom cleans up after me." Being the persistent person he is (with great intentions), my husband tried to coach and remind Ivaan of the same lesson yet again. This lasted for four calls. The fifth time we got on a FaceTime call, Ivaan said, "I don't think I want to talk to Uncle right now, maybe later." He had never said this before. Coming from a four-year-old, I was amazed as I reflected on the big lesson this little dude was imparting. Even kids only want to be reminded, coached, and taught things a few times, and unless they see value in it, they shut down. Isn't that true for grown-ups too? So much so. There is a subtle balance between what to say, when to say it, how much to say, and when to pause. Pausing is equally or arguably even more critical if you want to get the message across. There is a right time and place for everything, and we need to be ready to learn and understand.

Ivaan, thank you for this brilliant lesson. As they say, children can be our greatest teachers if we are humble enough to listen to them.

As I reflect upon my life, personal and professional, and draw from the experiences of others around me, I know that EQ is amongst the most critical skills that need to be taught early on in life. It's a key element to having a successful and fulfilling life. Although it's probably one of the most underrated skills, it's the one that takes you far in life, both personally and professionally.

It's about your ability to be clear-headed, present, calm under fire, and respond with your emotions cooled off. People with a high EQ are acutely aware of their current situation and the impact of their behavior. They can manage their feelings well and protect their relationships, perhaps even nurture them. Given that we can't change the past, we must use it to better our lives by reflecting upon situations after our emotions have cooled to understand what happened.

I sincerely hope this will allow you to see the role EQ plays in your life. Once you recognize the importance of EQ, it will help you get to know yourself better. That is the "bedrock" stuff. You can uncover your trigger points, frequency, patterns, and how you choose to handle them through continuous reflection. Selecting how you respond to situations and considering the consequences will allow you to see and evaluate your options. You are most likely looking at the next phase of your career and trying to figure out what is next for your career and life. Thinking about all you have learned, you will create a better next phase.

EQ is an acquired skill and can be cultivated by deliberate practice and repetition. Once you practice this muscle, you will be able to see what others can't.

Action

Carefully think about one particularly notable instance in your personal and professional life in which you "reacted versus responded." One in which you had the opportunity to pull the emotional aspect out of the conversation and make it fact-based. Elaborately write down the experience with intricate details of how you reacted and your impact on others around you.

What would you change, and how would you respond today? Remember, the point of this exercise is to unlearn previous methods and mechanisms to come up with solutions without being defensive and not give impractical judgments with the first thought that comes to mind in a raw, unfiltered reaction.

Understanding the atmosphere, the congregation, the occasion, and the time before coming back to speak is always a strategic and well thought out move. The truth is that we often react without thinking. It's our gut reaction based on fear and insecurities, but it's not the most rational or appropriate way to act. Respond based on the situation and select the best course of action based on values such as rationality, compassion, and cooperation.

CHAPTER TEN: HEAD, HEART AND HANDS SYNCHRONIZATION

Don't be your own prisoner. When one door closes, another opens, but you often look at the closed door for so long that you do not realize and appreciate the one that has opened. We are often our own prisoners, fighting with ourselves, trying to free our thoughts. Being happy and free comes from a place of peace and being in sync with yourself. This chapter will share three key elements crucial to unlocking this. When you believe this, you won't look back. You will continue moving forward, opening new doors, and doing new things as a result of being deeply in sync with yourself. At the end of the day, to live a fulfilling life, three elements need to be in harmony: your head, heart, and hands. The most important person you need to answer to is yourself. As long as you recognize you are giving your best with benevolence and integrity, that is all that matters. Most people walk this planet, often blinded to the big, beautiful world out there. When your imagination exceeds your reach, you see it. Our ability to be in sync with ourselves unleashes that. You will be able to see the forest instead of getting tangled up in the trees.

My parents have been my inspiration in life. Having been

extremely spiritual and religious people, they led by example. They taught me the value of these three elements cooperting.

My dad, to this day, wakes up at 4:00 am and meditates, followed by yoga, and then walks for miles. I didn't realize the impression it left on my subconscious growing up and how much it would affect my life as an adult. I became what I saw day in and day out. My mom has a heart of gold. She lives with an open heart to help people in need, and she does it in such a nonchalant way that no one would ever realize her generosity. I learned from her the skill of letting go and smiling no matter what. She always said God gave you two ears, one to listen with and the other to let go of what you choose to ignore. Don't let the unnecessary clutter go deep into your heart. Forgiving and forgetting, her mantra, could be so liberating and could be the free passage to freedom. Her key was to have a short-term memory for unpleasant moments and a photographic memory for pleasant ones. I never quite understood how she could operate like that nor how forgiveness could liberate you. I still have so much to learn from my parents. I aspire to live a life as holistically balanced as they do.

The beauty of life is that all three components play a crucial role in one's well-being. We don't realize it in our early adulthood, but as we grow, it seems evident that all the components are crucial. Pay attention to your patterns. How you learned to survive may not be how you want to continue living. Nourish your core: heal and shift, rinse and repeat.

A coach of mine, Sheila, once said something that struck a chord; "At twenty, we care what other people will think about us; at forty, we don't care as much what other people will think about us; at sixty, we realize that no one ever thought about us."

Mental and Emotional Well-Being

I was going through an extremely hectic schedule and was barely getting a chance to breathe. To say the least, it felt chaotic from within. Yet from the exterior, I needed to make it look okay. The mismatch of interior versus exterior was unsettling. I was neither the best nor at ease with myself when I needed to show something that was not in sync with what was going on within me. This unsettling feeling went on for months, maybe a year or so. I called my dad one fine day and talked to him about this uneasiness that was going on. He suggested I try meditation and see if it helped. That was the day, almost a decade ago now, I picked up this life-changing habit.

As I began my meditation journey, I struggled and wandered; I had to let the process take its time and not rush it. After all, this wasn't a light switch I was turning on or off. It made me feel better, and I appreciated and saw its benefits for my mental well-being. This fifteen-minute daily habit has made all the difference in my life. I developed an intrinsic ability to see things through a clear lens, which led me to make better decisions.

There have been numerous days when I had dozens of tasks overlapping, most of them involving a ton of ambiguity. That was and still is the norm in our world. Thanks to the power I developed with my fifteen-minute meditation, I could see things clearly and set my priorities with some unobstructed "next steps" and things I needed to focus on. How amazing is that?!

I figured out the framework of the most critical presentations during those fifteen minutes. It provided me with an entirely new perspective, which otherwise I wouldn't have. I wouldn't trade this for anything. I wish someone had taught me meditation and mindfulness early on in my life—whether it's stress, anxiety, or managing emotions, this is a potent tool. It will not solve all our problems, but it can certainly make us ten times more skillful in handling them. I earnestly hope it becomes a part of the school curriculum. I started practicing meditation for five minutes each day at five in the morning more than ten years ago. It was the best time of day as there was pin-drop silence in my home. I chose a comfortable, cozy loveseat, and turned the lights off. In the beginning, it was hard to sit still as my mind wandered in all directions. Despite being uneasy for several months, I committed myself to trying this. I let my mind wander wherever it was supposed to and didn't try to centralize it. I just let it become a free bird. Over a period of time, it settled on its own. It still wanders at times, even after a decade of meditating. Ultimately, meditation brought me incredible serenity and calmness.

A Few Things You Might Want to Consider as You Try This Practice:

- Believe in the power of meditation.
- Choose a comfortable spot—call it your zen zone.
- Choose a time to meditate and stick to it.
- Close your eyes.
- Start small—five minutes. Gradually increase it to ten or fifteen minutes at your own pace.
- Commit to doing it X number of times each week and stick to it.
- Give your mind permission to wander and be kind to it—don't judge.
- Don't resist distractions—in our heads, we mostly live in the past or the future (don't we?) - not in the present. If we learned to pause our past and future thoughts, we could choose what we'd like to focus on.

- Don't expect to see results right away. Ten-minute investments will pay off in the long run. You owe it to yourself.
- You will have a much healthier relationship with yourself and, by that virtue, with others.
- Meditation equals immense clarity, a difference in perspective, a sense of purpose, the ability to declutter, the knack to see things clearly amongst the chaos, and increased self-awareness.

Letting go = mental massage = mindfulness training.

> *"We know what we are but know not what we may be."*
> *– William Shakespeare*

Life always has a certain sense of mystery, a taste of surprise. Hence, let your mind rest from all uncertainty and unpredictability—what is meant to be will be.

You become what you think and feel.

Smoothen it UP

I had severe seasonal allergies for the first three decades of my life. During the spring and fall seasons, I had to take strong medications for weeks to get things under control. I was extremely tired of taking the medicine and having watery eyes, a runny nose, and headaches. I could barely open my eyes for weeks let alone days when it hit. Despite trying different remedies and having multiple doctor visits, it didn't seem like there was a cure for the issue, so I continued taking medications and getting shots periodically. A few years back, I was casually talking to a dear friend of mine, catching up on life. She was going through a significant life-changing event and was trying different plant-based diets. Her son was born with a limb-length discrepancy - painful beyond comprehension. It took my friend years to go through the stages of denial and achieve acceptance. Once she accepted reality, she wanted to make the most of the situation. She completely changed her and her family's lifestyle. Diet was a significant part of it.

As I listened to her, it gave me an idea to try and cure my allergies. I started with making fresh vegetable juice but couldn't sustain the work that came with it. Saving time was essential to me. Therefore, I pivoted to making smoothies - specifically green smoothies. It was months before I witnessed the benefits of curing my allergies. Since then, which was almost fifteen years ago now, I've rarely taken an allergy pill. All I needed to do was invest ten minutes every morning in making a healthy smoothie. It's a family habit now. My kids initially despised it, but you get what you get and don't throw a fit. They weren't given the option to choose. What you consume defines your mental and physical character. It not only helped my allergies heal from the core, but it also gave me physical strength, which made me feel better overall.

You become what you consume.

Conquer Your Fears: From Petrified to Pure Love

At the tender age of seven, I was bitten by a dog in the beautiful mountains of Nainital where I spent the first ten years of my life. Back then, especially in India, pet vaccinations weren't much of a thing, and there wasn't much public awareness or record keeping. As a result of this incident, I recall getting thirteen shots. It was horrendous and something that, even after decades, I still remember and feel. That incident left a permanent mark on me and created an untouchable fear of pets - especially dogs. My friends, throughout the years, have had to keep their pets in their basements or guarded areas whenever I visited them. However, a magical moment occurred during Christmas of 2020. My family and I were at a friend's place for a Christmas dinner, and everyone was encouraging me to pet their dog, Mojo, gently. Full of fear and anxiety, I decided to give it a try and pet Mojo. Within two months of that, on February 18, we got our first puppy. In honor of Senior Mojo, who passed away within this brief period due to illness, we named our dog Mojo. After all, Senior Mojo was the one who changed my life by taking away my fear. Our COVID puppy changed our lives forever. This instance again taught me that facing our fears can be rewarding and liberating. We need to let them go by reaching out to our fears and confronting them. Our limitations are our own. The same applies to our workplace. You fear speaking up, not being good enough, fear failure, fear sharing your opinion, or asking for help.

You cannot be courageous unless you're afraid because courage requires standing in the face of fear and doing it anyway. What fear have you stood in front of and conquered? Remember, great things lie right outside your comfort zone.

> *"You become what you face and conquer. You become what you think, what you consume, what you imagine, what you feel."*
> *– Shweta Bhatia*

To lead a fulfilling life, three components need to be in sync: your head that envisions the future and prioritizes it clearly;

your heart full of love, faith, compassion, and inspiration; and your hands to take incremental steps toward your future with agility. These three components need to become parallel to create a holistic, harmonized you. Take a pause, step back from everything, and spend time with yourself for some self-talk. The more time you spend with yourself consistently, the more you will be able to see what makes you happy and fulfilled. I invite you to join me by jotting down the intentions of your head, heart, and hands. These intentions will bring harmony to your being. Feeding your mind will improve your mental health. Filling your heart with love will accentuate gratitude and giving. Your hands will focus on the causes you care about with the hope of bringing true meaning and purpose. Keep adding to this as you uncover yourself through this process. It's there only to serve you.

A Cue for My Head, Heart, and Hands:

- Meditate often for emotional health.
- Expand your day by learning something new every day for your mental health.
- Make time to exercise for physical health.
- "Cleanse your brain" - get more sleep, and make it a non-negotiable ritual.
- Stay hydrated - it helps you think better.
- Consume less sugar and bad carbs.
- Spend quality time with family and friends.
- Let it go.
- Remove clutter from your life—emotionally, mentally, and physically.
- Do not respond to negativity.
- Laugh more often.
- Show more gratitude.

- Spread motivation and sunshine to others.
- Participate in more random acts of kindness - they matter.
- Be intentional about appreciating someone every day.
- Forgive first – it's a passage to freedom.
- If you see something beautiful in someone, say it.
- Your heart matters most.
- Love, live and keep faith.
- It is okay to not be liked by everyone. It means you are taking a stance for something you believe. Those who value what you do are your people, and the others don't belong on your journey.
- The most important person that you need to answer to is yourself. As long as you know you are doing the best you can with honesty and integrity for yourself and those around you, that is all that matters.

CHAPTER ELEVEN: CRAFTING THE RAINBOW OF LIFE

"Don't live the same year seventy-five times and call it a life."
– Robin Sharma

Everyone has an individuality, exceptionally endowed with opportunities and an extraordinarily unique life. It's up to you to pave your path and live a holistically fulfilling life. Your past is a page from history; the present and future are what you can influence and change. You have already accomplished the first step by embarking on this journey. Much appreciation and love to you for taking charge of your life and creating your story as you go. Remember that you are always a work in progress—I haven't met anyone who isn't, but sometimes, people don't consider themselves that way. You have the courage and power to take charge and craft your future. In your brilliant way, write the unwritten story.

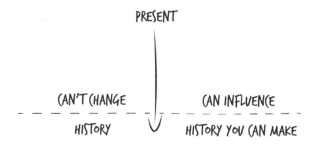

Your Thoughts + Actions = Manifestations

When you design your future story and take only a small step to set it in motion, even if you give only one percent to that dream, you will have accomplished it before you even know. Believing in your dreams and charting your future is the first crucial step. The goal of this book and the framework outlined is to help you live an enriching life: personally and professionally. My innate desire is to help you build, develop, and grow in all the facets that fill your lives with love, contentment, and happiness. It's building a life that you don't need to escape from regularly. I hope that by sharing snippets from my past failures, learnings, and experiences, I was able to and will continue to help you create your RAINBOW.

Remember, your limitations are entirely your own. You have to believe in yourself and try. You can do so much more than you ever thought you could. Recall the famous words of Vince Lombardi, "Winners never quit, and quitters never win." Keep moving forward with an open mind and a loving heart.

What We Think vs the Reality

In the following graph, you see your perception of success versus reality. Perception is how others view us, but reality embodies all the challenges you come across in your life. These challenges are authentically described in this book through various anecdotes and examples, with a practical framework to overcome them.

Pereception

What is appears to be

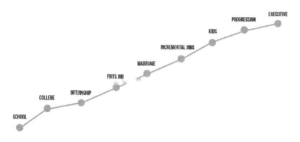

Reality

What the actual journey is

This book aims to help you change your mindset and live a fulfilling life through a well-thought-out and well-structured plan.

The seven-step RAINBOW process will help you change your mindset to live a fulfilled and accomplished life. You will gleam with confidence, feeling content with a sense of purpose and a plan to achieve new heights. You will feel a sense of fulfillment due to an expanded network and broader perspectives, which will open doors to several new opportunities and learnings. It's like being stuck in a small room in a house to having access to the entire house - the feeling of being liberated. You will become unstoppable in achieving anything that you set your mind to.

I often find myself reaching out and drawing the lessons from my RAINBOW box. In the future, when you are overwhelmed by your spiteful boss, being pulled down by a coworker, critiquing yourself for a suboptimal meeting outcome, or, have self-doubt, pull from your RAINBOW box, or draw inspiration from mine.

My Rainbow Box

- Start believing rather than seeing first, and you will start seeing things with a different lens – it will change your outlook.
- Give yourself permission without an iota of doubt. All the forces in the universe will align to make it happen – magic follows.
- Listen more than you speak.
- Spend time with just yourself.
- Be present in the moment—no matter what you are doing. It's the greatest gift to the other person.
- Listen to your intuition.
- Take chances.
- Have a no regret policy.
- Respond, don't react.
- Believe that you're always a work in progress.
- Never underestimate your skills.
- Don't take yourself too seriously. After all, you only have one life.
- Give more than you take.
- Be authentic – it takes too much effort to be something else, so why bother?
- Let it go.

- Character trumps everything.
- Pick your circle carefully.
- Uplift at least one person every day; everyone could use a warm hug, a friendly pat on the back, or a simple thank you.
- Know what to say and, more importantly, when to say it.
- Be gentle – the world will continue to turn without you.
- Be yourself—everyone else is taken.
- Fill the gaps in your EQ (emotional quotient), RQ (relationship quotient), SQ (social quotient), SQ (spiritual quotient), AQ (authentic quotient), and PQ (political quotient).

I hope you learn that it is possible to live the life of your dreams by taking control of your career through this process. Where you are right now is not a determining factor in your success. It's quite the contrary. It is simply a starting point from where you can better your life. However, you must remember that it is your responsibility to take action. You are the only person who can make these dreams come true. Of course, your journey may require help. It may need a loving yet firm hand to guide you through the tough times, but it is your responsibility to take that first empowering step toward success at the end of the day.

It is important to remember that you are not alone during your journey towards a better career and life. I've had my share of fears and trepidations; I did not have a godfather, nor did I have the conventional pedigree of a start-up founder. I trusted my gut and didn't let my doubts—or the doubters—hold me back. There are (unfortunately) an innumerable number of people out there right now experiencing something similar to what you are. I don't say this to scare you or make you think any complacent thoughts. Instead, I say that to empower you to take action now.

Everyone seeking success, wanting to take the right steps on the way, hopes that they receive guidance from someone who has already achieved the feat, but only a few are lucky enough to get the right advice from the right person. When that guardian angel who can point us in the right direction doesn't come along, many who want to make it big in life are left behind.

That is precisely why I want to let you know that I am here for you if you ever need some loving guidance. You can reach me at reimaginecareer@gmail.com.

Here is to a better you as you start this journey with me.

ACKNOWLEDGMENTS

It takes a village to accomplish anything, and this book is no different.

I'd like to thank my mentees, without whom even the thought of this book would not have been possible. The idea to write a book came from several of you; not even in my wildest dreams did I ever imagine it. So, with all my heart, I thank you. I have learnt from you equally or more in our journey together.

I want to thank my mentors and coaches who believed in me, took chances on me, and supported me when times were tough and I had doubts in myself. Thank you for endorsing me, boosting my credibility, and picking me up when I tripped. I will never forget your kindness.

Finally, this book is dedicated to aspiring professionals all over the world who face challenges and struggles as they prepare to go forth in their career. Although their journey may be challenged by pitfalls and obstacles, my sincere wish is that it be filled with hope, love, connection, spark and fulfillment. I hope that this book will assist them on their journey.

Beyond this broad group, some people deserve special thanks for their patience and help with this project.

Thank you, Jeff and Brian, for your steadfast support and wise counsel.

To my dear friend, Dr. Sunita Joshi, who pushed me not to overthink and start writing.

Shradha, I am so glad you came into my life. We have known each other not too long, but you have profoundly impacted me.

I am deeply grateful to my dear friend Ami for imparting some tough but necessary life lessons.

And my longest-lasting friend, Tina, who welcomed me into her heart and life and helped me settle in a new city, whose hospitality and friendship I will never forget.

To my sister, Anjali, who continuously encouraged me and kept me grounded. To my sister-in-law, Sonam, whose positive energy acted like a catalyst throughout the process. To my brother, Ankur, for always just being there and saying a million words without speaking much.

To my nephew, Aman, whose passion and brilliance continue to inspire me; and for his patience in going through many gyrations of the cover design.

To my mother-in-law and father-in-law; thank you for treating me like your daughter and for being a huge part of my support system.

Acknowledgments

To my husband, Mayank, who continually manages to share interesting ideas, challenges me to reinvent my thinking, and cheerfully dealt with a writing process that required me to sometimes disappear in order to finish my thought process.

To my daughter, Tanya, and son, Yuvraj, for remaining curious enough about the world, motivating me to observe more, not judge, and always listen with both ears. You both have been my greatest teachers. You three make my world complete.

Reinvent Your Career

ABOUT THE AUTHOR

Shweta Bhatia is a technology executive and leader with more than twenty years of experience as an entrepreneur and leader with many Fortune 500 companies. The recipient of the prestigious 40 under 40 award, her mission is to help aspiring professionals realize their full potential and reach their highest levels of fulfillment through coaching, counseling, and mentoring.

Made in United States
Orlando, FL
13 February 2023

29946437R00075